cooking school
Thai

cooking school

Thai

Bring the flavors of Thailand to life in your own kitchen!

LOVE FOOD is an imprint of Parragon Books Ltd

Parragon
Queen Street House
4 Queen Street
Bath BA1 1HE, UK

ISBN: 978-1-4075-9099-8

Printed in China

Design by Pink Creative
New recipes, introduction, and chapter opener text by Christine McFadden
Edited by Fiona Biggs
New photography (including front cover photography) by Clive Streeter
New home economy by Angela Drake

Notes for the Reader
This book uses imperial, metric, and US cup measurements. Follow the same units of
measurement throughout; do not mix imperial and metric. All spoon measurements are
level: teaspoons are assumed to be 5 ml, and tablespoons are assumed to be 15 ml.
Unless otherwise stated, milk is assumed to be whole, eggs and individual vegetables,
such as potatoes, are medium, and pepper is freshly ground white pepper.

The times given are an approximate guide only. Preparation times differ according to
the techniques used by different people and the cooking times may also vary from those
given as a result of the type of oven used. Optional ingredients, variations, or serving
suggestions have not been included in the calculations.

Recipes using raw or very lightly cooked eggs should be avoided by infants, the elderly,
pregnant women, convalescents, and anyone with a chronic condition. Pregnant and
breastfeeding women are advised to avoid eating peanuts and peanut products. People
with nut allergies should be aware that some of the prepared ingredients used in the
recipes in this book may contain nuts. Always check the packaging before use.

Contents

Introduction

The pleasure of cooking and eating is at the heart of Thai life. However, the Thais do not eat large amounts of food at any one meal. Instead, they nibble away at a variety of dishes throughout the day and night. Food is easy to come by—neighborhood restaurants, market stalls, and street vendors sell a fantastic selection of dishes at affordable prices.

Rice is key to the cuisine, so much so that the Thai equivalent of "How are you?" is "Have you had rice today?" It is the perfect foil for the typical Thai flavors—salty, hot, sour, and sweet—that give the cuisine its special character.

Regional Variations

With radical variations in topography and climate, ranging from cool mountainous peaks in the north to lush tropical forests in the south, the regions have distinctive cooking styles.

North Thailand

Bordering the southern Himalayas, this cool, remote area has limited grazing for cattle and relatively few waterways. Pork is therefore the preferred meat, while fish takes a back seat. Flavors are sharp, salty, and sour, rather than searingly hot. Broiled and deep-fried foods are popular, as is sticky rice sold steamed and wrapped in banana leaves.

Northeast Thailand

Hampered by poor soil and severe deforestation, the food of this region reflects the difficult conditions. Trademark flavors are simple but robust—huge amounts of chile, garlic, ginger, lime, and Thai fish sauce are used, tempered by generous portions of sticky rice. Because of the lack of fuel, raw or pickled foods, such as salt-preserved fish, are also a feature of the cuisine.

Central Thailand

This fertile, well-irrigated region lies at the economic and cultural heart of the country. The cooking is rich and complex, making lavish use of coconut milk, meat, freshwater fish, and shellfish, such as succulent shrimp and crayfish. Sweetness predominates, but is always balanced by a salty sour element and fiery chiles.

The food is the best known outside Thailand, thanks to the large numbers who emigrated from the region and set up restaurants around the world. It is what we think of as typically Thai and includes pad Thai and the familiar red and green curries.

South Thailand

The food of this slender peninsula is the spiciest and most strongly flavored in Thailand. Exceptionally hot Thai chiles, sour tamarind, unripe fruit, and astringent herbs and spices are tamed by the richness of coconut—both the cream and the oil that is widely used for frying. With many miles of coastline, fish and shellfish are a feature of the cuisine.

Mutton, beef, and chicken are popular meats, reflecting the influence of the Thai Muslims who, for religious regions, do not eat pork.

Tips on Menu Planning

A basic Thai meal consists of rice accompanied by a soup, a curry, a zesty salad, and a vegetable dish. Dessert is a concept that does not exist in Thailand, although fresh fruit might finish off the meal.

You can cook as few or as many dishes as you like. It's always best to master two or three simple ones before moving on to a more ambitious menu. As a rule of thumb for a sharing menu, plan one dish per person plus rice.

Tips and Techniques

Before starting to cook

Assemble all the ingredients, then measure them as necessary. Complete any initial preparation, such as grating and chopping. Cut fresh ingredients into small, equal-size pieces so that they cook in the same amount of time. Shredding vegetables thinly and slicing them diagonally increases the surface area in contact with the hot oil and speeds up cooking. Line up the prepared ingredients in bowls, ready to add to the pan at the correct time.

Preparing spices

Always use whole spices and grind them as needed. Once ground or crushed, they quickly lose their distinctive aroma and flavor. Before grinding, dry-fry whole spices without any oil to coax out maximum flavor. Thai cooks use white peppercorns rather than black. These are not dry-fried because doing so imparts a bitter flavor.

Stir-frying

Make sure the wok is very hot before you add the oil—hold your hand flat about 2¾ inches/7 cm above the bottom of the wok until you feel the heat. Use a long-handled ladle or tongs to stir the ingredients constantly so that they all come in contact with the hot oil and are evenly cooked.

Deep-frying

Thai cooks use less oil for deep-frying than Western cooks. Use enough to create a depth of about 1 inch/2.5 cm. Heat it over medium–high heat until a faint haze appears. If the oil is not hot enough, the food will soak it up and become soggy. Cook in small batches to avoid overcrowding the pan. Remove the food with tongs and drain on paper towels.

Cooking Equipment

You don't need special equipment to produce authentic Thai food. However, the following items are important.

MORTAR AND PESTLE

The most indispensable item is a large mortar and pestle, preferably made from rough stone, such as granite. Thai cooks use them for grinding, crushing, or mashing spices, fresh herbs, fibrous roots, and other ingredients to make relishes and curry pastes.

SPICE GRINDER

A small spice grinder (or electric coffee grinder kept especially for the purpose) is useful for grinding large amounts of spices.

WOK

With its conical shape, the wok is the best pan to use for stir-frying. Thanks to the outward-sloping sides, the food continually falls back to the center where the heat is most intense. If fitted with a lid and a stand for stability, the wok can also be used for curries and deep-fried dishes. A heavy-bottom, deep-sided skillet can be substituted for a wok.

Ingredients

You will need basic seasonings, oils, and various other pantry items, many of which you will already have. Commonly used ingredients, such as limes, fresh ginger, garlic, and coconut milk, are easily found in supermarkets. The more unusual items are sold in Thai stores, by mail order, or—for creamed coconut, for example—on the internet. It's worth stocking up with these as they will give your cooking that authentic Thai flavor.

Unopened cans and jars will keep for months in a pantry and for several weeks in the refrigerator once opened. Fresh items, such as kaffir lime leaves, cilantro root, and galangal can all be frozen until needed.

CHILES

Thai chiles are small and incredibly hot. The very hottest are the "mouse-dropping" chiles, which are about ½ inch/1 cm long. Almost as hot are the slightly larger Thai chiles. Red chiles are riper versions of green ones and are marginally milder. Chiles will keep for several weeks stored in a plastic bag in the refrigerator.

CILANTRO ROOT

Asian stores sell big bunches of fresh cilantro with the roots attached. Don't throw these away—they are a vital ingredient in sauces and curry pastes. If not needed immediately, cut off the leaves and store the roots in a sealed plastic bag in the freezer.

CREAMED COCONUT

Unlike coconut cream, this is sold as a solid block from which you can simply shave off what you need.

EGGPLANTS

Thai eggplants are different from the purple Mediterranean variety. There are three types: Marble-size green "pea" eggplants, slightly larger oval white ones, and the round green "apple" eggplant. They are all clean tasting and crisp, and are eaten raw or lightly cooked. If necessary, diced purple eggplant can be used instead, but the texture will be softer and the color lacking.

THAI FISH SAUCE

Known as "nam pla" in Thailand, fish sauce is a thin brown liquid made by fermenting fish with salt. It has a pungent, almost rotten aroma, but adds a special richness and flavor to foods. It is diluted in dipping sauces and is used at the table in the same way as salt.

GALANGAL

Recognizable by its translucent gold skin, galangal is used in the same way as ginger but has a sharper, more peppery flavor. Found mainly in Asian stores, the fresh root can be stored in the refrigerator for several weeks or frozen until needed. Chopped galangal is sold in jars but the flavor is inferior to that of the fresh root.

KAFFIR LIME LEAVES

These are glossy dark green leaves that grow in pairs. They have a unique lemon-lime flavor and are used in the same way as bay leaves. Fresh or frozen leaves have a much better flavor than dried.

LEMONGRASS

This lemon-scented grass has a cool refreshing flavor that counteracts the heat of chiles. It has a long woody stalk with fibrous leaves and a white bulbous stem end. Peel away the coarse outer layers before chopping or pounding.

PALM SUGAR

Sold in disks, cones, or cylinders, palm sugar has a rich caramel-like flavor. It is used not just in sweet dishes, but also in savory dishes to counteract the saltiness of soy and fish sauce and to temper the heat of chiles. If it is hard, use a vegetable peeler to shave off small pieces.

SHRIMP PASTE

Made from a particular kind of fermented, salted, and sun-dried shrimp, this imparts an essential Thai flavor to curry pastes, marinades, and sauces. Don't be put off by the overpowering aroma—it disappears once heated. Keep the paste in a very well-sealed container in the refrigerator.

Thai Curries

Thailand is justly famous for its fresh-tasting curries, made from aromatic pastes of mashed chiles, fresh herbs and roots, fish sauce, and other seasonings. The classics are green curry, red curry, the sweet-sour "masaman" curry, and the milder Penang curry. Curry pastes are sold already made (look for the Thai brands sold in Thai stores) but it's hard to beat homemade pastes for flavor and vibrant color. They can be kept in a screw-top jar in the refrigerator for up to a week.

GREEN CURRY PASTE
Makes ¾ cup

1 tbsp coriander seeds

½ tbsp cumin seeds

1 tsp white peppercorns, crushed

4 tbsp water

12 Thai chiles, seeded and chopped

5 garlic cloves, chopped

2 lemongrass stalks, coarse outer leaves discarded, chopped

5 fresh or frozen kaffir lime leaves, chopped

1¼ cups fresh cilantro, chopped

finely grated rind of 1 lime

Heat a skillet until hot, add the coriander seeds, and dry-fry over medium–high heat, shaking the pan frequently, for 2 minutes, or until starting to pop. Remove from the skillet and reserve, then add the cumin seeds to the skillet and dry-fry for 30 seconds, or until fragrant, being careful not to let them burn.

Grind the toasted seeds and the peppercorns to a coarse powder, using a mortar and pestle. Put the powder and all the remaining ingredients into a blender and process for 2–3 minutes to a thick, smooth paste, scraping down the pitcher several times. Transfer to a screw-top glass jar and store in the refrigerator for up to a week.

RED CURRY PASTE
Makes ¾ cup

12 dried red chiles, seeded

1 tbsp coriander seeds

½ tbsp cumin seeds

1 tsp white peppercorns, crushed

6 tbsp water

2 shallots, chopped

1-inch/2.5-cm piece fresh ginger, chopped

2 lemongrass stalks, coarse outer leaves discarded, chopped

4 fresh or frozen kaffir lime leaves, chopped

1 tbsp chopped cilantro root or 1 extra tsp coriander seeds

finely grated rind of 1 lime

1 tsp salt

Put the chiles in a small bowl, cover with boiling water, and let soak for 15 minutes, until pliable. Drain and set aside.

Heat a skillet until hot, add the coriander seeds, and dry-fry over medium–high heat, shaking the pan frequently, for 2 minutes, or until starting to pop. Remove from the skillet and reserve, then add the cumin seeds to the skillet and dry-fry for 30 seconds, or until fragrant, being careful not to let them burn.

Grind the toasted seeds and the peppercorns to a coarse powder, using a mortar and pestle. Put the powder and all the remaining ingredients into a blender and process for 2–3 minutes to a thick, smooth paste, scraping down the pitcher several times. Transfer to a screw-top glass jar and store in the refrigerator for up to a week.

Soups and Appetizers

Thai meals are not divided into separate courses as they are in the West. Soups and small dishes with which we would normally begin the meal are put on the table along with all the other dishes.

Since there is no prescribed order of eating, soups are enjoyed throughout the meal and are used to balance flavors. For example, Hot-and-Sour Soup would be good before or after a meat dish with a sweet flavor, and the simple Pork and Vegetable Broth would counteract the richness of a masaman curry. Substantial noodle soups, such as Spicy Shrimp Soup, are meals in themselves and can be served Western-style with nothing more than a zesty salad.

Thais also enjoy eating a selection of small dishes with drinks, served well before the main meal in order not to spoil the appetite. "Appetizers" are also eaten at any time of day—first thing in the morning, as a mid-morning snack, or as a mid-afternoon pick-me-up.

Typical small dishes include delectable Crispy Sesame Shrimp and Crab Cakes. There are also irresistible satays, spicy wontons, and spring rolls. These are, in fact, Chinese in origin, but have spread throughout Southeast Asia. They are surprisingly substantial and on their own would make an excellent meze meal for sharing with friends, or even a Thai-style Sunday brunch.

Beef and Noodle Soup

SERVES 4

4 shallots, chopped

1 large garlic clove, chopped

2 tsp finely chopped fresh ginger

1 tbsp peanut oil

1 lb/450 g sirloin steak, external fat
   removed, cut into ½-inch/1-cm cubes

5¼ cups beef stock

1 tsp white peppercorns, crushed

5½ oz/150 g flat rice noodles

juice of 1 lime

2 tsp Thai fish sauce

½ tsp salt

½ tsp sugar

TO GARNISH

4 scallions, shredded

slivers of fresh red chile

3 tbsp torn cilantro leaves

3 tbsp torn basil leaves

lime wedges

1. Puree the shallots, garlic, and ginger in a food processor or blender, pulsing several times, until a fairly smooth paste forms.

2. Heat a wok over medium–high heat, then add the oil. Add the paste and stir-fry for 2 minutes, being careful to avoid letting it burn. Add the beef and stir-fry for 1 minute, until brown, then pour in 4 cups of the stock. Bring to a rapid boil, skimming off any foam that forms. Add the crushed peppercorns, then reduce the heat and gently simmer for 30–35 minutes, or until the meat is tender.

3. Meanwhile, cook the noodles according to the package directions.

4. When the meat is tender, stir in any sticky residue that has formed at the edge of the wok. Add the remaining stock, the lime juice, fish sauce, salt, and sugar. Simmer for a few minutes.

5. Drain the noodles and divide among warmed soup bowls. Ladle the meat and broth over the top. Serve immediately with the garnishes sprinkled over the soup.

Pork and Vegetable Broth

SERVES 4

1 tbsp chili oil

1 garlic clove, chopped

3 scallions, sliced

1 red bell pepper, seeded and
   finely sliced

2 tbsp cornstarch

4 cups vegetable stock

1 tbsp soy sauce

2 tbsp rice wine or dry sherry

5½ oz/150 g pork tenderloin, sliced

1 tbsp finely chopped lemongrass

1 small red chile, seeded and
   finely chopped

1 tbsp grated fresh ginger

4 oz/115 g fine egg noodles

7 oz/200 g canned water chestnuts,
   drained and sliced

salt and pepper

1. Heat a large pan, then add the oil. Add the garlic and scallions and cook over medium heat, stirring, for 3 minutes, until slightly softened. Add the bell pepper and cook for an additional 5 minutes, stirring.

2. In a bowl, mix the cornstarch with enough of the stock to make a smooth paste and stir it into the pan. Cook, stirring, for 2 minutes. Stir in the remaining stock, the soy sauce, and rice wine, then add the pork, lemongrass, chile, and ginger. Season to taste with salt and pepper. Bring to a boil, then reduce the heat and simmer for 25 minutes.

3. Cook the noodles according to the package directions. Remove from the heat, drain, then add to the soup along with the water chestnuts. Cook the soup for an additional 2 minutes, then remove from the heat, ladle into warmed bowls, and serve immediately.

Chicken Noodle Soup

SERVES 4

1 tbsp sesame oil or chili oil

2 garlic cloves, chopped

2 scallions, trimmed and sliced

1 leek, trimmed and finely sliced

1 tbsp grated fresh ginger

1 red chile, seeded and finely chopped

12 oz/350 g skinless, boneless chicken
   breasts, cut into strips

scant 3½ cups chicken stock

2 tbsp rice wine

1 tbsp chopped lemongrass

6 kaffir lime leaves, finely shredded

7 oz/200 g fine egg noodles

salt and pepper

1. Heat a wok, then add the oil. Add the garlic and cook over medium heat, stirring, for 1 minute, then add the scallions, leek, ginger, and chile and cook, stirring, for another 3 minutes. Add the chicken, stock, and rice wine, bring to a boil, and simmer for 20 minutes. Stir in the lemongrass and lime leaves.

2. Cook the noodles according to the package directions. Remove from the heat, drain, then add them to the soup. Season with salt and pepper to taste. Cook for an additional 2 minutes. Remove from the heat, ladle into warmed serving bowls, and serve hot.

Chicken-Coconut Soup

SERVES 4

4 oz/115 g dried cellophane noodles

5 cups chicken stock or vegetable stock

1 lemongrass stalk, crushed

½-inch/1-cm piece fresh ginger, peeled and very finely chopped

2 fresh kaffir lime leaves, thinly sliced

1 fresh red chile, or to taste, seeded and thinly sliced

2 skinless, boneless chicken breasts, thinly sliced

1 cup coconut cream

2 tbsp Thai fish sauce

1 tbsp fresh lime juice

½ cup bean sprouts

4 scallions, green part only, finely sliced

fresh cilantro leaves, to garnish

1. Cook the noodles according to the package directions. Remove from the heat, drain, and set aside.

2. Meanwhile, bring the stock to a boil in a large pan over high heat. Reduce the heat, add the lemongrass, ginger, lime leaves, and chile and let simmer for 5 minutes. Add the chicken and continue simmering for an additional 3 minutes, or until cooked. Stir in the coconut cream, fish sauce, and lime juice and continue simmering for 3 minutes. Add the bean sprouts and scallions and simmer for an additional minute. Taste and gradually add extra fish sauce or lime juice, if needed. Remove and discard the lemongrass stalk.

3. Divide the noodles among warmed bowls. Bring the soup back to a boil, then ladle into the bowls. The heat of the soup will warm the noodles. Sprinkle with cilantro leaves and serve immediately.

Duck and Scallion Soup

SERVES 2

2 duck breasts, skin on

2 tbsp Red Curry Paste (see page 11)

2 tbsp vegetable oil or peanut oil

bunch of scallions, chopped

2 garlic cloves, crushed

2-inch/5-cm piece fresh ginger, grated

2 carrots, thinly sliced

1 red bell pepper, seeded and cut into strips

4 cups chicken stock

2 tbsp sweet chili sauce

3–4 tbsp soy sauce

14 oz/400 g canned straw mushrooms, drained

1. Slash the skin of the duck three or four times with a sharp knife and rub in the curry paste. Cook the duck breasts, skin-side down, in a wok or skillet over high heat for 2–3 minutes. Turn over, reduce the heat, and cook for an additional 3–4 minutes, until cooked through. Lift out and slice thickly. Set aside and keep warm.

2. Meanwhile, heat a wok over medium–high heat, then add the oil. Add half the scallions, the garlic, ginger, carrots, and bell pepper and stir-fry for 2–3 minutes. Pour in the stock and add the chili sauce, soy sauce, and mushrooms. Bring to a boil, reduce the heat, and simmer for 4–5 minutes.

3. Ladle the soup into warmed bowls, top with the duck slices, and garnish with the remaining scallions. Serve immediately.

Spicy Shrimp Soup

SERVES 4

1 tbsp corn oil

2–3 garlic cloves, cut into thin slivers

1–2 fresh red chiles, seeded and sliced

2 lemongrass stalks, outer leaves removed, chopped

1-inch/2.5-cm piece fresh ginger, grated

2½ cups fish stock or vegetable stock

12 oz/350 g large shrimp, peeled and deveined

4 oz/115 g shiitake mushrooms, sliced

1 large carrot, grated

2 oz/55 g dried egg noodles (optional)

1–2 tsp Thai fish sauce

1 tbsp chopped fresh cilantro, plus a few sprigs to garnish

1. Heat a large pan over medium heat, then add the oil. Add the garlic, chiles, lemongrass, and ginger and cook for 5 minutes, stirring frequently. Add the stock and bring to a boil, then reduce the heat and let simmer for 5 minutes.

2. Stir in the shrimp, mushrooms, and carrot. If using the egg noodles, break into small lengths, add to the pan, and let simmer for an additional 5 minutes, or until the shrimp have turned pink and the noodles are tender.

3. Stir in the fish sauce and cilantro and heat the soup through for 1 minute before serving, garnished with cilantro sprigs.

Tom Yum Soup with Fish

SERVES 6

5½ cups light chicken stock

6 lemongrass stalks, crushed to release their flavor

3 tbsp very finely chopped cilantro root

10 kaffir lime leaves, central stalks torn off

1 red chile, seeded and finely chopped

1-inch/2.5-cm piece galangal or fresh ginger, peeled and thinly sliced

3 tbsp Thai fish sauce

1 tbsp sugar

1 lb 2 oz/500 g shrimp, peeled except for the tails

1 lb 2 oz/500 g firm white fish, such as cod or monkfish, chopped into bite-size pieces

8 oz/225 g canned bamboo shoots or water chestnuts

12 cherry tomatoes, halved

juice of 2 limes

handful of fresh cilantro leaves and handful of fresh Thai basil leaves, chopped, plus a few whole leaves to garnish

1. Pour the stock into a large pan and add the lemongrass, cilantro roots, lime leaves, chile, galangal, fish sauce, and sugar. Cover the pan. Bring to a boil, then reduce the heat and simmer for 10 minutes.

2. Add the shrimp, fish, and bamboo shoots and simmer for an additional 4 minutes. Add the tomatoes and lime juice and check the seasoning, adding more fish sauce and sugar, if necessary.

3. Remove and discard the lemongrass stalks, then divide the soup among warmed bowls, scatter over the cilantro and basil leaves, and serve immediately.

Hot-and-Sour Soup

SERVES 4

2 fresh red chiles, seeded
  and coarsely chopped

6 tbsp rice vinegar

5 cups vegetable stock

2 lemongrass stalks, halved

4 tbsp soy sauce

1 tbsp light brown sugar

juice of ½ lime

2 tbsp vegetable oil or peanut oil

1¼ cups drained and cubed firm tofu

14 oz/400 g canned straw mushrooms,
  drained

4 scallions, chopped,
  plus extra to garnish

1 small head bok choy, shredded,
  to garnish

1. Mix the chiles and vinegar together in a nonmetallic bowl. Cover and let stand at room temperature for 1 hour.

2. Meanwhile, bring the stock to a boil in a pan. Add the lemongrass, soy sauce, sugar, and lime juice, then reduce the heat and simmer for 20–30 minutes.

3. Heat a wok over high heat, then add the oil. Add the tofu cubes and stir-fry for 2–3 minutes, or until browned all over. (You may need to do this in two batches, depending on the size of the wok.) Remove with a slotted spoon and drain on paper towels.

4. Add the chiles and vinegar with the tofu, mushrooms, and half the scallions to the stock mixture and cook for 10 minutes. Mix the remaining scallions with the bok choy, sprinkle over the soup, and serve immediately.

Spicy Beef and Mushroom Wontons

MAKES 12–15

12–15 square wonton wrappers

peanut oil, for deep-frying

soy-ginger dipping sauce, to serve

FILLING

4 oz/125 g ground sirloin or top
round steak

1 scallion, green part included,
finely chopped

2 button mushrooms, finely chopped

1 small garlic clove, finely chopped

½ tsp finely chopped fresh ginger

½ tsp soy sauce

¼ tsp salt

¼ tsp pepper

⅛ tsp Chinese five-spice seasoning

½ tsp cornstarch

½ egg, beaten

1. To make the filling, combine the steak, scallion, mushrooms, garlic, and ginger in a
   bowl. Mix the soy sauce, salt, pepper, five-spice seasoning, and cornstarch to a thin
   paste. Add the paste to the beef mixture, then stir in the beaten egg.

2. Separate the wonton wrappers and place on a tray, rotating them so one corner
   is facing toward you. Cover with a clean, damp dish towel to prevent them from
   drying out. Working with one wrapper at a time, place a slightly rounded teaspoon
   of filling in the bottom corner, ½ inch/1 cm away from the point. Fold the point
   over the filling, then roll up two-thirds of the wrapper, leaving a point at the top.
   Moisten the right- and left-hand corners with a dab of water. Fold one corner over
   the other and press lightly to seal into a bishop's miter shape. Continue until all the
   wontons are filled.

3. Heat a large wok over high heat, then add the oil and heat to 350–375°F/
   180–190°C, or until a cube of bread browns in 30 seconds. Add the wontons in
   batches and deep-fry for 4–5 minutes, or until golden brown. Remove with tongs
   and drain on crumpled paper towels. When they are all cooked, serve immediately
   with the dipping sauce.

Crispy Pork Dumplings

SERVES 4

3 scallions, coarsely chopped

1 garlic clove, coarsely chopped

1 small fresh red chile, seeded and
coarsely chopped

9 oz/250 g ground pork

1 tsp salt

20 wonton wrappers

peanut oil or vegetable oil, for deep-
frying

chile flowers, to garnish

1. To make the dumplings, put the scallions, garlic, chile, pork, and salt into a food processor and process to a smooth paste.

2. Remove the wonton wrappers from the package, but keep them covered with a clean, damp dish towel to prevent them from drying out. Lay one wrapper on a counter in front of you in a diamond shape and brush the edges with water. Put a small amount of filling near one edge and fold the wrapper over the filling. Press the edges together to seal the parcel and shape into a semicircle. Repeat with the remaining wrappers and filling.

3. Heat a large wok over high heat, then add the oil and heat to 350–375°F/180–190°C, or until a cube of bread browns in 30 seconds. Add the dumplings, in batches, and cook for 45 seconds–1 minute, or until crisp and golden all over. Remove with a slotted spoon and drain on paper towels, then keep warm while you cook the remaining dumplings. When they are all cooked serve immediately, garnished with chile flowers.

Pork and Shrimp Egg Rolls

MAKES 25

6 dried Chinese mushrooms, soaked in warm water for 20 minutes

1 tbsp vegetable oil or peanut oil, plus extra for deep-frying

8 oz/225 g ground pork

1 tsp dark soy sauce

8 oz/225 g fresh or canned bamboo shoots, rinsed and julienned (if using fresh shoots, boil in water first for 30 minutes)

pinch of salt

3½ oz/100 g shrimp, peeled, deveined, and chopped

1⅔ cups coarsely chopped, fresh bean sprouts

1 tbsp finely chopped scallion

25 egg roll wrappers

1 egg white, lightly beaten

chili sauce, to serve

1. Squeeze out any excess water from the mushrooms and finely slice, discarding any tough stems.

2. To make the filling, heat a wok over medium–high heat, then add the oil. Add the pork and stir-fry, until it changes color. Add the soy sauce, bamboo shoots, mushrooms, and salt. Stir over high heat for 3 minutes.

3. Add the shrimp and cook for 2 minutes, then add the bean sprouts and cook for an additional minute. Remove from the heat and stir in the scallion. Let cool.

4. Place a tablespoon of the filling toward the bottom of a wrapper. Roll once to secure the filling, then fold in the sides to create a 4-inch/10-cm-long egg roll and continue to roll up. Seal with egg white.

5. Heat a large wok over high heat. Add the oil and heat to 350–375°F/180–190°C, or until a cube of bread browns in 30 seconds. Cook the egg rolls, in batches, for about 5 minutes, until golden brown and crispy. Serve immediately with chili sauce.

Chicken Satay Skewers

SERVES 4

4 skinless, boneless chicken breasts, about 4 oz/115 g each, cut into ¾-inch/2-cm cubes

4 tbsp soy sauce

1 tbsp cornstarch

2 garlic cloves, finely chopped

1-inch/2.5-cm piece fresh ginger, peeled and finely chopped

cucumber, coarsely chopped, to serve

PEANUT SAUCE

2 tbsp peanut oil or vegetable oil

½ onion, finely chopped

1 garlic clove, finely chopped

4 tbsp crunchy peanut butter

4–5 tbsp water

½ tsp chili powder

1. Put the chicken cubes in a shallow dish. Mix the soy sauce, cornstarch, garlic, and ginger together in a small bowl and pour over the chicken. Cover and let marinate in the refrigerator for at least 2 hours. Meanwhile, soak 12 bamboo skewers in cold water for at least 30 minutes.

2. Preheat the oven to 375°F/190°C. Divide the chicken cubes between the bamboo skewers. Heat a ridged grill pan until hot, then add the skewers and cook over high heat for 3–4 minutes, turning occasionally, until browned all over. Transfer the skewers to a baking sheet and cook in the preheated oven for 5–8 minutes, or until cooked through.

3. Meanwhile, to make the sauce, heat a wok over medium heat, then add the oil. Add the onion and garlic and cook, stirring frequently, for 3–4 minutes, or until softened. Add the peanut butter, water, and chili powder and let simmer for 2–3 minutes, or until softened and thinned.

4. Serve the skewers immediately with the warm peanut sauce and the cucumber.

Crab Cakes

SERVES 6

10½ oz/300 g canned crabmeat, drained

1–2 fresh Thai chiles, seeded and finely chopped

6 scallions, trimmed and thinly sliced

¾ cup grated zucchini

scant 1½ cups peeled and grated carrot

1 tbsp chopped fresh cilantro

2 tbsp cornstarch

2 egg whites

1 spray corn oil

⅔ cup lowfat plain yogurt

Tabasco sauce, to taste

2 tsp sesame seeds

lime wedges, to garnish

1. Place the crabmeat in a bowl and stir in the chile, scallions, zucchini, carrot, and cilantro. Add the cornstarch and mix well.

2. Beat the egg whites together in a separate bowl, then stir into the crab mixture and mix together.

3. Heat a nonstick skillet over low heat, then lightly spray with the oil. Drop small spoonfuls of the crab mixture into the skillet and fry for 3–4 minutes, pressing down with the back of a spatula. Turn the crab cakes over halfway through cooking. Cook in batches.

4. Mix the yogurt and Tabasco sauce in a small bowl and stir in the sesame seeds. Spoon into a small bowl and use as a dipping sauce with the cooked crab cakes. Serve garnished with lime wedges, divided equally among six plates.

Crispy Sesame Shrimp

SERVES 4

generous ¾ cup self-rising flour

3 tbsp sesame seeds, toasted or
dry-fried

1 tsp Red Curry Paste
(see page 11)

1 tbsp Thai fish sauce

⅔ cup water

vegetable oil or peanut oil, for
deep-frying

20 large shrimp, peeled,
with tails intact

chili sauce, for dipping

sprigs of fresh cilantro, to garnish

1. Combine the flour and sesame seeds in a bowl. Stir the curry paste, fish sauce, and water together in a pitcher, until mixed. Gradually pour the liquid into the flour, stirring continuously, to make a thick batter.

2. Heat a large wok over high heat. Add the oil and heat to 350–375°F/180–190°C, or until a cube of bread browns in 30 seconds. Holding the shrimp by their tails, dip them into the batter, one at a time, then carefully drop into the hot oil. Cook for 2–3 minutes, until crispy and brown. Drain on paper towels.

3. Serve immediately with chili sauce, garnished with cilantro sprigs.

Spicy Parcels

SERVES 4

OMELETS	FILLING
4 eggs	1 tbsp peanut oil
2 tbsp water	3 scallions, coarsely chopped
3 scallions, finely chopped	8 oz/225 g squid, cleaned and cut into chunks if large or rings if small
small handful of fresh cilantro, finely chopped	4 oz/115 g shrimp, peeled and deveined
peanut oil or vegetable oil, for frying	4 oz/115 g skinned white fish fillet, such as cod or coley, cut into 1-inch/2.5-cm cubes
soy sauce, to serve	1 head bok choy, coarsely chopped
	1 tbsp Green Curry Paste (see page 11)
	1 tsp Thai fish sauce

1. Preheat the oven to 375°F/190°C. For the omelets, beat the eggs, water, scallions, and half the cilantro together in a bowl. Heat 1 tablespoon of oil in an 8-inch/20-cm nonstick skillet. Drizzle a quarter of the egg mixture over the bottom of the skillet to make a rough lacy pattern. Cook over medium–high heat for 2 minutes, or until just set, then use a spatula to turn the omelet over and cook on the other side for 1 minute. Slide out onto a plate or cutting board. Repeat with the remaining mixture to make three more omelets and add to the plate or board.

2. For the filling, heat a wok over medium heat, then add the oil. Add the scallions and all the seafood and cook, stirring frequently, for 2–3 minutes, or until the squid is firm, the shrimp have turned pink, and the fish is just cooked through. Transfer to a food processor and process for 30 seconds, or until just mixed. Add the bok choy, the remaining cilantro, the curry paste, and fish sauce and process again to a coarse mixture.

3. Arrange the omelets on a cutting board and put a quarter of the seafood mixture in the center of each. Roll one side of each omelet over the filling and fold in the adjacent "sides" to cover the filling, then fold up the omelet to make a small, square parcel. Transfer the parcels to a baking sheet.

4. Bake in the preheated oven for 10–15 minutes, or until lightly browned and cooked through. Serve immediately with soy sauce.

Vegetable and Black Bean Egg Rolls

SERVES 4

2 tbsp peanut oil or vegetable oil, plus extra for deep-frying

4 scallions, cut into 2-inch/5-cm lengths and shredded lengthwise, plus extra to garnish

1-inch/2.5-cm piece fresh ginger, peeled and finely chopped

1 large carrot, peeled and cut into thin sticks

1 red bell pepper, seeded and cut into thin sticks

6 tbsp black bean sauce

⅓ cup fresh bean sprouts

7 oz/200 g canned water chestnuts, drained and coarsely chopped

2-inch/5-cm piece cucumber, cut into thin sticks

8 egg roll wrappers, 8-inch/20-cm square

sweet chili dipping sauce, to serve (optional)

1. Heat a wok over medium–high heat, then add the oil. Add the scallions, ginger, carrot, and bell pepper and stir-fry for 2–3 minutes. Add the black bean sauce, bean sprouts, water chestnuts, and cucumber and stir-fry for 1–2 minutes. Let cool.

2. Remove the egg roll wrappers from the package, but keep them covered with a clean, damp dish towel to prevent them from drying out. Lay one wrapper on a counter in front of you in a diamond shape and brush the edges with water. Put a spoonful of the filling near one corner and fold the corner over the filling. Roll over again and then fold the side corners over the filling. Roll up to seal the filling completely. Repeat with the remaining wrappers and filling.

3. Heat a large wok over high heat, then add enough oil for deep-frying and heat to 350–375°F/180–190°C, or until a cube of bread browns in 30 seconds. Add the rolls, in 2–3 batches, and cook for 2–3 minutes, or until crisp and golden all over. Remove with a slotted spoon and drain on paper towels, then keep warm while you cook the remaining rolls. When they are all cooked, garnish with shredded scallions and serve immediately with sweet chili dipping sauce, if using.

Vegetables and Salads

Thanks to the varying climate, Thailand produces an impressive variety of vegetables, many of which are used in the West and some that are not so familiar. Cooked or raw vegetables accompany every meal, mitigating the heat of chiles and providing welcome texture and color.

Cabbages, cucumber, and carrots are popular, either raw in salads and relishes, or lightly cooked in a stir-fry. There are various types of green beans: Winged beans, which taste something like asparagus, and yard-long, or asparagus beans, which are similar in flavor to ordinary green beans. Thai "pea" eggplants and round "apple" eggplants are a key ingredient, adding color and crunch to stir-fries and curries. Freshness is paramount, and every part of the vegetable, including shoots and roots that Western cooks might discard, is put to good use.

Unlike the soft leafy salads of the West, Thai salads are an exciting mix of substantial ingredients with bold flavors and distinct textures. Beef and poultry often form the basis, as do oily fish, such as tuna—try the mouthwatering Caramelized Tuna Salad or the zesty Gingered Chicken and Vegetable Salad. Sharp-tasting fruits, such as pomelo (a type of grapefruit) and green mango, also feature.

Dressings range from the clean sharp flavors of lime juice, Thai fish sauce, and chile, to more complex concoctions, which may include ginger and sesame oil. Fresh herbs, such as mint, cilantro, and basil, are used in abundance rather than as a sprinkling over a finished dish.

Mixed Vegetables with Basil

SERVES 4

2 tbsp vegetable oil or peanut oil, plus extra for shallow-frying

2 garlic cloves, chopped

1 onion, sliced

1 cup baby corn, halved diagonally

½ cucumber, peeled, halved, seeded, and sliced

8 oz/225 g canned water chestnuts, drained and rinsed

generous ¾ cup snow peas

2 cups shiitake mushrooms, halved

1 red bell pepper, seeded and thinly sliced

1 tbsp light brown sugar

2 tbsp light soy sauce

1 tbsp Thai fish sauce

1 tbsp rice vinegar

8–12 sprigs fresh Thai basil

cooked plain rice, to serve

1. Heat a wok over high heat, then add the oil. Add the garlic and onion and stir-fry for 1–2 minutes. Add the baby corn, cucumber, water chestnuts, snow peas, mushrooms, and bell pepper and stir-fry for 2–3 minutes, until they begin to soften.

2. Add the sugar, soy sauce, fish sauce, and vinegar and gradually bring to a boil. Let simmer for 1–2 minutes.

3. Meanwhile, heat a separate wok over high heat, then add enough oil for shallow-frying. Add the basil sprigs and cook for 20–30 seconds, until crisp. Remove with a slotted spoon and drain on paper towels.

4. Garnish the vegetable stir-fry with the crispy basil and serve immediately with cooked rice.

Broccoli with Peanuts

SERVES 4

3 tbsp vegetable oil or peanut oil

1 lemongrass stalk, coarsely chopped

2 fresh red chiles, seeded and chopped

1-inch/2.5-cm piece fresh ginger, grated

3 kaffir lime leaves, coarsely torn

3 tbsp Green Curry Paste
(see page 11)

1 onion, chopped

1 red bell pepper, seeded and chopped

1 large head broccoli, cut into florets

1 cup green beans

scant ½ cup unsalted peanuts

1. Put 2 tablespoons of the oil, the lemongrass, chiles, ginger, lime leaves, and curry paste into a food processor or blender and process to a paste.

2. Heat a wok over medium heat, then add the remaining oil. Add the spice paste, onion, and bell pepper and stir-fry for 2–3 minutes, until the vegetables start to soften.

3. Add the broccoli and beans, cover, and cook over low heat, stirring occasionally, for 4–5 minutes, until tender.

4. Meanwhile, toast or dry-fry the peanuts, until lightly browned. Add them to the broccoli mixture and toss together. Serve immediately.

Cauliflower and Beans with Cashew Nuts

1 tbsp vegetable oil or peanut oil

1 tbsp chili oil

1 onion, chopped

2 garlic cloves, chopped

2 tbsp Red Curry Paste
  (see page 11)

1 small cauliflower, cut into florets

2 cups sliced yard-long beans

⅔ cup vegetable stock

2 tbsp Thai soy sauce

scant ⅓ cup toasted cashew nuts,
  to garnish

1. Heat a wok over medium–high heat, then add the vegetable oil and the chili oil. Add the onion and garlic and stir-fry, until softened. Add the curry paste and stir-fry for 1–2 minutes.

2. Add the cauliflower and beans and stir-fry for 3–4 minutes, until softened. Pour in the stock and soy sauce and let simmer for 1–2 minutes. Serve immediately, garnished with the cashew nuts.

Mushroom and Tofu Laksa with Noodles

SERVES 4

3½ cups vegetable stock

1¾ cups coconut milk

9 oz/250 g shiitake mushrooms, stalks removed, thinly sliced

1 cup cubed firm tofu

2 tbsp tomato paste

6 oz/175 g fine egg noodles

salt and pepper

sliced scallions and shredded cabbage, to garnish

SPICE PASTE

2 fresh red chiles, seeded and chopped

1½-inch/4-cm piece fresh ginger, chopped

2 large garlic cloves, chopped

2 lemongrass stalks, tough outer layers discarded, inner stalks chopped

1 tsp coriander seeds, crushed

6 macadamia nuts, chopped

8 cilantro roots with short length of stem attached, or small handful of fresh cilantro

3 tbsp vegetable oil

1. Puree the spice paste ingredients in a food processor, pulsing several times, until smooth.

2. Heat a wok over medium–high heat, add the spice paste, and stir-fry for 30 seconds. Pour in the stock and coconut milk and bring to a boil. Add the mushrooms, tofu, and tomato paste and season with salt and pepper to taste. Simmer gently for 5 minutes.

3. Meanwhile, cook the noodles according to the package directions. Divide among four large soup bowls. Ladle the spicy broth over the noodles and serve immediately, garnished with sliced scallions and shredded cabbage.

Vegetable Stir-Fry

SERVES 4

2 tbsp peanut oil or vegetable oil

1 bunch of scallions, coarsely chopped

1-inch/2.5-cm piece fresh ginger, peeled and finely chopped

2 lemongrass stalks, halved

2 carrots, peeled and cut into thin sticks

1 small head broccoli, cut into florets

scant ½ cup baby corn, halved lengthwise

2 oz/55 g canned water chestnuts, drained

1 tbsp Red Curry Paste (see page 11)

8 oz/225 g dried medium egg noodles

4 tbsp sesame seeds

1. Heat a wok over medium–high heat, then add the oil. Add the scallions, ginger, and lemongrass and stir-fry for 2–3 minutes, or until starting to soften. Add the carrots, broccoli, and baby corn and stir-fry for 3–4 minutes, until starting to soften. Add the water chestnuts and curry paste and stir well, then stir-fry for an additional 2–3 minutes. Discard the lemongrass.

2. Meanwhile, cook the noodles according to the package instructions, until just tender. Drain and return to the pan. Add the sesame seeds and toss to coat.

3. Add the noodles to the stir-fried vegetables and serve immediately.

Red Curry with Mixed Leaves

SERVES 4

2 tbsp peanut oil or vegetable oil

2 onions, thinly sliced

1 bunch of fine asparagus spears

1¾ cups coconut milk

2 tbsp Red Curry Paste
(see page 11)

3 fresh kaffir lime leaves

8 oz/225 g baby spinach leaves

2 heads bok choy, chopped

1 small head Chinese cabbage,
shredded

handful of fresh cilantro, chopped

cooked plain rice, to serve

1. Heat a wok over medium–high heat, then add the oil. Add the onions and
    asparagus and stir-fry for 1–2 minutes.

2. Add the coconut milk, curry paste, and lime leaves and bring gently to a boil,
    stirring occasionally. Add the spinach, bok choy, and Chinese cabbage and cook,
    stirring, for 2–3 minutes, or until wilted. Add the cilantro and stir well. Serve
    immediately with rice.

Spring Vegetable Rice

SERVES 4

2 tbsp peanut oil or vegetable oil

2 shallots, chopped

2 garlic cloves, crushed

generous 1 cup basmati rice

2½ cups chicken stock

1 tbsp Red Curry Paste
  (see page 11)

1 tsp Thai fish sauce

3 tbsp soy sauce

1½ cups baby corn, halved lengthwise

8 large baby carrots, halved lengthwise

scant 1 cup snow peas

⅓ cup fresh bean sprouts

4 tbsp sesame seeds

handful of fresh cilantro, chopped

2 tbsp sesame oil

salt

1. Heat a wok over medium–high heat, then add the peanut oil. Add the shallots and garlic and stir-fry for 1–2 minutes. Add the rice and stir-fry for 2–3 minutes. Add the stock, curry paste, fish sauce, and soy sauce and bring to a boil, stirring occasionally. Reduce the heat and simmer for 10–12 minutes, or until the rice is tender, adding more stock or boiling water, if necessary,

2. Meanwhile, bring a pan of lightly salted water to a boil, add the baby corn and carrots, and cook for 2–3 minutes, or until just tender. Add the snow peas and cook for 1 minute. Add the bean sprouts and stir well, then drain.

3. Heat a dry skillet over medium–high heat, then add the sesame seeds and cook, shaking the skillet frequently, for 30–45 seconds, or until lightly browned.

4. Add the drained vegetables, cilantro, and sesame oil to the rice and serve immediately, sprinkled with the toasted sesame seeds.

Carrot and Pumpkin Curry

SERVES 4

⅔ cup vegetable stock

1-inch/2.5-cm piece fresh galangal, sliced

2 garlic cloves, chopped

1 lemongrass stalk (white part only), finely chopped

2 fresh red chiles, seeded and chopped

4 carrots, peeled and cut into chunks

2 cups peeled, seeded, and cubed pumpkin

2 tbsp vegetable oil or peanut oil

2 shallots, finely chopped

3 tbsp Thai yellow curry paste

1¾ cups coconut milk

4–6 fresh Thai basil sprigs

2 tbsp toasted pumpkin seeds, to garnish

1. Pour the stock into a large pan and bring to a boil. Add the galangal, half the garlic, the lemongrass, and chiles and let simmer for 5 minutes. Add the carrots and pumpkin and let simmer for 5–6 minutes, until tender.

2. Meanwhile, heat a wok over medium–high heat, then add the oil. Add the shallots and the remaining garlic and stir-fry for 2–3 minutes. Add the curry paste and stir-fry for 1–2 minutes.

3. Stir the shallot mixture into the pan and add the coconut milk and basil. Let simmer for 2–3 minutes. Serve hot, sprinkled with the toasted pumpkin seeds.

Tofu and Vegetable Curry

SERVES 4

2 tbsp vegetable oil or peanut oil,
  plus extra for deep-frying

1¼ cups drained and cubed firm tofu

2 onions, chopped

2 garlic cloves, chopped

1 fresh red chile, seeded and sliced

3 celery stalks, diagonally sliced

3¼ cups thickly sliced mushrooms

1 cup baby corn, halved

1 red bell pepper, seeded and
  cut into strips

3 tbsp Red Curry Paste
  (see page 11)

1¾ cups coconut milk

1 tsp light brown sugar

2 tbsp Thai soy sauce

5 cups baby spinach leaves

1. Heat a wok over high heat, then add enough oil for deep-frying and heat to 350–375°F/180–190°C, or until a cube of bread browns in 30 seconds. Add the tofu cubes, in batches, and deep-fry for 4–5 minutes, until crispy and browned. Remove with a slotted spoon and drain on paper towels.

2. Heat a separate wok over medium–high heat, then add 2 tablespoons of oil. Add the onions, garlic, and chile and stir-fry for 1–2 minutes, until they start to soften. Add the celery, mushrooms, corn, and bell pepper and stir-fry for 3–4 minutes, until they soften.

3. Stir in the curry paste and coconut milk and gradually bring to a boil. Add the sugar and soy sauce and then the spinach. Cook, stirring continuously, until the spinach has wilted. Serve immediately, topped with the tofu.

Cabbage and Coconut Curry

SERVES 4–6

3 tbsp vegetable oil

1 tsp mustard seeds

1 small onion sliced

¼ white cabbage, core removed, leaves shredded

½ small green cabbage, core removed, leaves shredded

⅓–½ cup water

½ tsp crushed white peppercorns

4 tbsp unsweetened dried toasted coconut flakes

3 tbsp chopped cilantro

juice of ½ lime

salt

SPICE PASTE

1¾ oz/50 g creamed coconut, melted

1 green chile, seeded and roughly chopped

1 tbsp finely chopped fresh ginger

2 garlic cloves, sliced

1 small onion, finely chopped

½ tsp salt

1 tsp cumin seeds

½ tsp ground turmeric

1. Puree the spice paste ingredients in a food processor or blender, adding a splash of water to moisten.

2. Heat a wok over medium–high heat, then add the oil. Add the mustard seeds and fry, until they start to crackle. Reduce the heat to medium, then add the onion and stir-fry, until golden. Stir in the spice paste and stir-fry for 30 seconds.

3. Add the shredded cabbages and pour in the water, stirring well so the cabbages are covered with the paste. Season with the crushed peppercorns and a little salt. Cover and cook over low heat for 7–10 minutes, stirring occasionally to prevent it from sticking.

4. When the cabbages are tender, add the coconut flakes, cilantro, and lime juice. Stir for a minute to heat through and serve immediately.

Peppered Beef Salad

SERVES 4

4 beef tenderloins, about
    4 oz/115 g each

2 tbsp black peppercorns, crushed

1 tsp Chinese five-spice seasoning

¾ cup bean sprouts

1-inch/2.5-cm piece fresh ginger,
    finely chopped

4 shallots, finely sliced

1 red bell pepper, seeded and
    thinly sliced

3 tbsp Thai soy sauce

2 fresh red chiles, seeded and sliced

½ lemongrass stalk, finely chopped

3 tbsp vegetable oil or peanut oil

1 tbsp sesame oil

lime halves, to garnish

1. Preheat the broiler to medium–high. Wash the steaks and pat dry on paper towels. Mix the peppercorns with the seasoning and press onto all sides of the steaks. Cook under the preheated broiler for 2–3 minutes each side, or until cooked to your liking.

2. Meanwhile, mix the bean sprouts, half the ginger, the shallots, and bell pepper together and divide among four plates. Mix the remaining ginger, soy sauce, chilies, lemongrass, vegetable oil, and sesame oil together.

3. Slice the beef and arrange on the vegetables. Drizzle with the dressing and serve immediately, garnished with lime halves.

Gingered Chicken and Vegetable Salad

SERVES 4

4 skinless, boneless chicken breasts

4 scallions, chopped

1-inch/2.5-cm piece fresh ginger, finely chopped

4 garlic cloves, 2 crushed and 2 chopped

3 tbsp vegetable oil or peanut oil

1 onion, sliced

1 cup baby corn, halved

1½ cups snow peas, halved lengthwise

1 red bell pepper, seeded and sliced

3-inch/7.5-cm piece cucumber, peeled, seeded, and sliced

4 tbsp Thai soy sauce

1 tbsp light brown sugar

a few Thai basil leaves

6 oz/175 g fine egg noodles

1. Cut the chicken into 1-inch/2.5-cm cubes. Mix the scallions, ginger, crushed garlic, and 1 tablespoon of the oil together in a shallow dish. Add the chicken. Cover and let marinate for at least 3 hours. Lift the meat out of the marinade and set aside.

2. Heat a wok over medium heat, then add the remaining oil. Add the onion and cook for 1–2 minutes, then add the chopped garlic, baby corn, snow peas, and bell pepper. Cook for 2–3 minutes, until just tender. Add the cucumber, half the soy sauce, the sugar, and the basil, and mix gently.

3. Cook the noodles according to the package directions, then drain well. Sprinkle the remaining soy sauce over them and arrange on plates. Top the noodles with the cooked vegetables.

4. Add a little more oil to the wok if necessary and cook the chicken over fairly high heat, until browned on all sides. Arrange the chicken cubes on top of the salad and serve hot or warm.

Red Chicken Salad

SERVES 4

4 boneless chicken breasts

2 tbsp Red Curry Paste
(see page 11)

2 tbsp vegetable oil or peanut oil

1 head napa cabbage, shredded

1 cup bok choy, torn into large pieces

½ savoy cabbage, shredded

2 shallots, finely chopped

2 garlic cloves, crushed

1 tbsp rice wine vinegar

2 tbsp sweet chili sauce

2 tbsp Thai soy sauce

1. Score the chicken several times and rub the curry paste into each cut. Cover and let chill overnight.

2. When ready to cook, heat a wok over medium heat, then add the chicken and cook for 5–6 minutes, turning once or twice, until cooked through. Keep warm.

3. Heat a separate wok, then add 1 tablespoon of the oil. Add the napa cabbage, bok choy, and savoy cabbage and stir-fry, until just wilted. Add the remaining oil, shallots, and garlic, and stir-fry, until just tender but not browned. Add the vinegar, chili sauce, and soy sauce. Remove from the heat.

4. Arrange the stir-fried leaves on four serving plates. Slice the chicken, arrange on top, and drizzle the hot dressing over the dish. Serve immediately.

Duck Salad

SERVES 4

4 boneless duck breasts, skin on

1 lemongrass stalk, broken into three
and each cut in half lengthwise

3 tbsp vegetable oil or peanut oil

2 tbsp sesame oil

1 tsp Thai fish sauce

1 fresh green chile, seeded and
chopped

2 tbsp Red Curry Paste
(see page 11)

½ fresh pineapple, peeled and sliced

3-inch/7.5-cm piece cucumber, peeled,
seeded, and sliced

3 tomatoes, cut into wedges

1 onion, thinly sliced

cilantro, to garnish

DRESSING

juice of 1 lemon

2 garlic cloves, crushed

1 tsp brown sugar

2 tbsp vegetable oil or peanut oil

1. Unwrap the duck and let the skin dry out overnight in the refrigerator.

2. The following day, slash the skin side five or six times. Mix the lemongrass,
2 tablespoons of the vegetable oil, the sesame oil, fish sauce, chile, and curry paste
together in a shallow dish and place the duck breasts in the mixture. Turn to coat
and rub the marinade into the meat. Let chill for 2–3 hours.

3. Heat a wok over medium heat, then add the remaining oil. Add the duck, and
cook, skin-side down, for 3–4 minutes, until the skin is browned and crispy and
the meat is cooked most of the way through. Turn the breasts over and cook, until
browned and cooked to your liking.

4. Meanwhile, arrange the pineapple, cucumber, tomatoes, and onions on a platter.
Mix the dressing ingredients together and pour over the top.

5. Lift the duck out of the wok and slice thickly. Arrange the duck slices on top of the
salad and serve while still hot, garnished with a few leaves of fresh cilantro.

Sea Bass and Mango Salad

SERVES 2

2 small sea bass, cleaned

1 tbsp Red Curry Paste
  (see page 11)

small handful of fresh cilantro, chopped

⅔ cup coconut milk

2 tbsp sweet chili sauce

6–8 Thai basil leaves, chopped

½ tsp Thai fish sauce

1 tsp rice wine vinegar

1 mango, seeded, peeled, and sliced

selection of mixed salad greens,
  to serve

1. Place the fish on a cutting board. Mix the curry paste and cilantro together and stuff inside each fish cavity. Cover and let marinate for 1–2 hours.

2. Preheat the oven to 400°F/200°C. Place the fish in a roasting pan. Mix the coconut milk, chili sauce, basil, fish sauce, and vinegar and pour over the fish. Arrange the mango slices in the pan. Cover with foil, place in the preheated oven, and cook for 15 minutes.

3. Remove the foil and cook, uncovered, for an additional 10–15 minutes, until the fish is cooked.

4. Place the fish on two warmed serving plates, drizzle with the cooking sauces, and serve immediately with the mixed salad greens.

Caramelized Tuna Salad

SERVES 4

2 cups fresh bean sprouts

4-inch/10-cm piece cucumber

1½ cups cilantro leaves

1½ cups mint leaves

1 tsp sesame oil, plus a few drops for drizzling

1 tbsp peanut oil

1 lb/450 g fresh tuna, cut into 1-inch/2.5-cm chunks

salt

2 tbsp salted roasted peanuts, crushed, to garnish

DRESSING

2 tsp canola oil

1 tsp finely chopped fresh ginger

½–1 small fresh red chile, seeded and finely chopped

4 tbsp light soy sauce

1 tbsp Thai fish sauce

1 tbsp tamarind paste

⅓ cup brown sugar

1. To make the dressing, heat a small wok over high heat, then add the oil. Add the ginger and chile and fry for a few seconds. Add the soy sauce, fish sauce, and tamarind paste. Stir for 30 seconds, then add the sugar and stir until dissolved. Remove the wok from the heat and set aside.

2. Rinse the bean sprouts in boiling water and drain. Blot dry with paper towels. Peel the cucumber, halve lengthwise, and scoop out the seeds. Thinly slice the flesh diagonally.

3. Put the bean sprouts, cucumber, cilantro, and mint leaves in a bowl. Season with a pinch of salt and drizzle with a few drops of sesame oil. Toss to combine, then divide among individual serving plates.

4. Heat a large wok over high heat, then add the sesame oil and peanut oil. Add the tuna and quickly stir-fry, turning with tongs, until colored on the outside but still slightly red in the middle. Arrange the tuna chunks on top of the salad.

5. Reheat the dressing, thinning with a spoonful of water if necessary, and pour over the tuna. Sprinkle with the crushed peanuts and serve immediately.

Hot-and-Sour Vegetable Salad

SERVES 4

2 tbsp vegetable oil or peanut oil

1 tbsp chili oil

1 onion, sliced

1-inch/2.5-cm piece fresh ginger, grated

1 small head broccoli,
cut into florets

2 carrots, cut into short thin sticks

1 red bell pepper, seeded and cut into
squares

1 yellow bell pepper, seeded and cut
into thin pieces

¾ cup halved snow peas

scant ½ cup baby corn, halved

DRESSING

2 tbsp vegetable oil or peanut oil

1 tsp chili oil

1 tbsp rice wine vinegar

juice of 1 lime

½ tsp Thai fish sauce

1. Heat a wok over high heat, then add the vegetable oil and chili oil. Add the
   onion and ginger and sauté for 1–2 minutes, until they begin to soften. Add the
   vegetables and stir-fry for 2–3 minutes, until they have softened slightly. Remove
   from the heat and set aside.

2. Mix the dressing ingredients together. Transfer the vegetables to a serving plate
   and drizzle the dressing over. Serve warm or let the flavors develop and serve cold.

Meat

Although meat features widely in Thai cuisine, it plays a less important role than in the West. In Thailand, meat is often just a component of a dish containing several other ingredients, and the dish itself is one of several served at a meal. However, there are plenty of meat-based dishes to be enjoyed, including classic curries, such as Coconut Beef Curry, lip-smacking roasts, and zesty cold dishes, such as Beef with Black Pepper and Lime, a dish originating from neighboring Malaysia.

Thailand boasts more recipes for pork than any other meat. It is cooked in every imaginable way—in soups and salads, curries and kebabs, stir-fries and snacks. Immensely popular in northern Thailand, and obligatory with relishes and curries, is crisp and puffy deep-fried pork skin, the Thai equivalent of pork cracklings. Also irresistible and eaten almost everywhere,

is sweet crispy pork, in which sugar plays a vital role in balancing excessively hot, sharp, and salty flavors, which in turn counteract the richness of the pork.

Although pork is a favorite meat throughout most of Thailand, the Muslim community in the south exclude it from the diet for religious reasons. Here, lamb and mutton are popular and beef is also eaten. With its rich distinctive flavor, lamb stands up to the spices in the typically hearty red curries. It is also excellent with refreshing herbal flavors, as in Green Lamb Stir-Fry with Noodles and Mint and Lamb with Lime Leaves.

Masaman Curry

SERVES 4

2 tbsp peanut oil or vegetable oil

1½ cups coarsely chopped shallots

1 garlic clove, crushed

1 lb/450 g beef tenderloin, thickly sliced and then cut into 1-inch/ 2.5-cm cubes

2 tbsp masaman curry paste

3 potatoes, peeled and cut into 1-inch/2.5-cm cubes

1¾ cups coconut milk

2 tbsp soy sauce

⅔ cup beef stock

1 tsp light brown sugar

½ cup unsalted peanuts

handful of fresh cilantro, chopped

noodles or cooked rice, to serve

1. Heat a wok over medium–high heat, then add the oil. Add the shallots and garlic and stir-fry for 1–2 minutes, or until softened. Add the beef cubes and curry paste and stir-fry over high heat for 2–3 minutes, or until browned all over. Add the potatoes, coconut milk, soy sauce, stock, and sugar and bring gently to a boil, stirring occasionally. Reduce the heat and simmer for 8–10 minutes, or until the potatoes are tender.

2. Meanwhile, heat a dry skillet over medium–high heat, then add the peanuts and cook, shaking the skillet frequently, for 2–3 minutes, or until lightly browned. Add to the curry with the cilantro and stir well. Serve hot with noodles.

Coconut Beef Curry

SERVES 4

1 tbsp ground coriander

1 tbsp ground cumin

3 tbsp masaman curry paste

scant 1 cup coconut cream

1 lb/450 g beef tenderloin,
   cut into strips

1¾ cups coconut milk

½ cup unsalted peanuts, finely chopped

2 tbsp Thai fish sauce

1 tsp light brown sugar

4 kaffir lime leaves

cooked rice, to serve

1. Combine the coriander, cumin, and curry paste in a bowl. Pour the coconut cream into a pan and bring just to a boil. Add the curry paste mixture and let simmer for 1 minute.

2. Add the beef and let simmer for 6–8 minutes, then add the coconut milk, peanuts, fish sauce, and sugar. Let simmer gently for 15–20 minutes, until the meat is tender.

3. Add the lime leaves and let simmer for 1–2 minutes. Serve hot with rice.

Marinated Beef with Celery

SERVES 4

1 lb 2 oz/500 g beef tenderloin,
   cut into thin strips

1 cup vegetable oil

3 celery stalks, cut into
   1-inch/2.5-cm thin strips

1 red bell pepper, cut into thin strips

1 red chile, seeded and finely sliced

lime wedges, to garnish

cooked rice and Thai fish sauce,
   to serve

MARINADE

1 tsp salt

2 tbsp Thai fish sauce

1. To make the marinade, mix the salt and fish sauce in a large bowl.

2. Add the beef and toss to coat. Cover with plastic wrap and put in the refrigerator
   for 1 hour to marinate.

3. Heat a wok over medium heat, then add the oil and heat to 350–375°F/180–190°C,
   or until a cube of bread browns in 30 seconds. Add the beef and deep-fry for
   2–3 minutes, or until crispy. Remove the wok from the heat and, using a slotted
   spoon, lift out the meat and drain it on paper towels. Discard all but 2 tablespoons
   of the oil.

4. Reheat the reserved oil in the wok, add the celery, bell pepper, and chile, and stir-
   fry for 1 minute. Add the beef and cook, until hot.

5. Garnish with lime wedges and serve immediately with rice and fish sauce.

Beef with Black Pepper and Lime

SERVES 2–3

12 oz/350 g flank steak

½ tbsp light brown sugar

1 tbsp black peppercorns, crushed

4 tsp soy sauce

1 red Thai chile, seeded and finely chopped

½ head garlic, cloves crushed

2 tbsp lime juice

½ head Chinese cabbage, sliced

½ red onion, thinly sliced

1½ tbsp peanut oil

½ tsp Thai fish sauce

3 tbsp chopped fresh mint

lime wedges, to garnish

cooked plain rice, to serve (optional)

1. Pound the steak with the blunt side of a knife. Slice diagonally across the grain into thin, bite-size pieces and put in a shallow bowl.

2. Combine the sugar, peppercorns, soy sauce, chile, garlic, and half the lime juice in a bowl, mixing well. Pour over the beef, stirring to coat. Marinate at room temperature for 1 hour, or overnight in the refrigerator.

3. Arrange the Chinese cabbage in a shallow serving dish. Scatter with onion slices.

4. Heat a wok over high heat, then add the oil. Add the beef and stir-fry for 3 minutes. Add the fish sauce and remaining lime juice, and stir-fry for an additional minute.

5. Add the meat and juices to the Chinese cabbage and onion, then scatter over the mint. Garnish with lime wedges and serve immediately with rice, if using.

Hot Beef and Coconut Curry

SERVES 4

1¾ cups coconut milk

2 tbsp Red Curry Paste
   (see page 11)

2 garlic cloves, crushed

1 lb 2 oz/500 g braising steak

2 fresh kaffir lime leaves, shredded

3 tbsp lime juice

2 tbsp Thai fish sauce

1 large fresh red chile, seeded and
   sliced

½ tsp ground turmeric

2 tbsp chopped fresh basil leaves

2 tbsp chopped cilantro leaves

salt and pepper

unsweetened dried shredded coconut,
   to garnish

freshly cooked rice, to serve

1. Place the coconut milk in a large pan and bring to a boil. Reduce the heat and simmer gently for 10 minutes, or until it has thickened. Stir in the curry paste and garlic and simmer for an additional 5 minutes.

2. Cut the beef into ¾-inch/2-cm chunks. Add to the pan and bring to a boil, stirring continuously. Reduce the heat and add the lime leaves, lime juice, fish sauce, chile, turmeric, and ½ teaspoon of salt.

3. Cover the pan and continue simmering for 20–25 minutes, or until the meat is tender, adding a little water if the sauce looks too dry.

4. Stir in the basil and cilantro and season with salt and pepper to taste. Sprinkle with shredded coconut and serve immediately with rice.

Pad Thai

SERVES 4

8 oz/225 g thick dried rice noodles

2 tbsp peanut oil or vegetable oil

4 scallions, coarsely chopped

2 garlic cloves, crushed

2 fresh red chiles, seeded and sliced

8 oz/225 g pork tenderloin, trimmed and thinly sliced

4 oz/115 g cooked, peeled jumbo shrimp

juice of 1 lime

2 tbsp Thai fish sauce

2 eggs, beaten

⅓ cup fresh bean sprouts

handful of fresh cilantro, chopped

⅓ cup unsalted peanuts, chopped

1. Cook the noodles according to the package directions, until just tender. Drain, then rinse under cold running water and set aside.

2. Heat a wok over medium–high heat, then add the oil. Add the scallions, garlic, and chiles and stir-fry for 1–2 minutes. Add the pork and stir-fry over high heat for 1–2 minutes, or until browned all over.

3. Add the shrimp, lime juice, fish sauce, and eggs and stir-fry over medium heat for 2–3 minutes, or until the eggs have set and the shrimp are heated through.

4. Add the bean sprouts, most of the cilantro, the peanuts, and the noodles and stir-fry for 30 seconds, or until heated through. Serve immediately, garnished with the remaining cilantro.

Caramelized Belly Pork with Star Anise

SERVES 2–3

1 lb 2 oz/500 g boneless pork belly

2 tbsp soy sauce

1 cup brown sugar

4 tbsp Thai fish sauce

1 tbsp oyster sauce

2 tbsp peanut oil

3 tbsp crisp-fried onion (from a jar)

2 tbsp chopped fresh cilantro

lime wedges, to garnish

SPICE PASTE

3 star anise pods

1 tsp coriander seeds or chopped fresh cilantro root

2 tsp white peppercorns

4 garlic cloves, crushed

salt

1. Trim the rind but not the fat from the belly pork. Put the meat in a shallow dish and sprinkle with the soy sauce. Cover and let marinate in the refrigerator for 1–24 hours.

2. For the spice paste, dry-fry the star anise pods and coriander seeds for 2 minutes, until fragrant. Combine with the remaining spice paste ingredients and grind, until smooth, using a mortar and pestle.

3. Bring a saucepan of water to a boil and steam the pork over the boiling water for 15 minutes. Reserve the liquid and let the meat cool. Slice into ¾-inch/2-cm strips, then rub in the paste.

4. Put the sugar, fish sauce, and oyster sauce in a pan. Stir over medium heat, until the sugar has dissolved.

5. Heat a wok over medium–high heat, then add the oil. Add the pork and stir-fry, until beginning to color. Sprinkle with a spoonful of the reserved cooking liquid if the meat starts to stick. Add the sugar mixture and stir for a few minutes, until it is bubbling and caramelized and the meat is well coated. Sprinkle with the fried onion and cilantro and serve immediately, garnished with lime wedges.

Red Pork Curry with Bell Peppers

SERVES 4

2 tbsp vegetable oil or peanut oil

1 onion, coarsely chopped

2 garlic cloves, chopped

1 lb/450 g pork tenderloin, thickly sliced

1 red bell pepper, seeded and cut into squares

2½ cups quartered button mushrooms

2 tbsp Red Curry Paste (see page 11)

2½ cups coconut cream

1 tsp pork or vegetable bouillon powder

2 tbsp Thai soy sauce

4 tomatoes, peeled, seeded, and chopped

handful of fresh cilantro, chopped

1. Heat a wok over medium–high heat, then add the oil. Add the onion and garlic and sauté for 1–2 minutes, until they are softened but not browned.

2. Add the pork slices and stir-fry for 2–3 minutes, until browned all over. Add the bell pepper, mushrooms, and curry paste.

3. Add the coconut cream to the wok with the bouillon powder and soy sauce. Bring to a boil and let simmer for 4–5 minutes, until the liquid has reduced and thickened.

4. Add the tomatoes and cilantro and cook for 1–2 minutes. Serve immediately.

Pork Stir-Fry with Cashew Nuts, Lime, and Mint

SERVES 2

10 oz/280 g pork tenderloin

1 tsp coriander seeds

½ tsp white peppercorns

¼ tsp salt

¼ tsp sugar

juice and finely grated rind of 1 lime

2 tbsp peanut oil

1 tsp finely chopped fresh ginger

1 garlic clove, thinly sliced

3 scallions, white and green parts
  separated, then halved lengthwise
  and sliced into ¾-inch/2-cm pieces

1 small green bell pepper, seeded and
  thinly sliced

2 tbsp coarsely chopped cashew nuts

large pinch of salt

1 tbsp chicken stock

1 tsp Thai fish sauce

2 tbsp coarsely chopped fresh mint,
  to garnish

1. Slice the pork across the grain diagonally into thin, bite-size pieces. Flatten with the back of a knife blade and spread out on a plate. Using a mortar and pestle, crush the coriander seeds, peppercorns, ¼ teaspoon of salt, sugar, and lime rind together. Spread the mixture over both sides of the pork, pressing it in well. Let stand for 15 minutes.

2. Heat a wok over high heat, then add 1 tablespoon of the oil. Add the pork and stir-fry for 2–3 minutes, until no longer pink. Transfer to a plate with the juices. Wipe the wok clean with paper towels.

3. Heat the wok over medium–high heat, then add the remaining oil. Add the ginger and garlic and stir-fry for a few seconds. Add the white parts of the scallions and the bell pepper and stir-fry for 2 minutes. Add the cashew nuts and pinch of salt, then stir-fry for an additional minute.

4. Increase the heat, then return the pork and juices to the wok. Add the stock, lime juice, fish sauce, and the green parts of the scallions. Stir-fry for 30 seconds to heat through, then sprinkle with the mint and serve immediately.

Red Roasted Pork with Peppered Noodles

SERVES 2

1 tbsp Red Curry Paste (see page 11)

2 tbsp soy sauce

12 oz/350 g piece pork tenderloin, trimmed

8 oz/225 g fine dried egg noodles

2 tbsp peanut oil or vegetable oil

1 red onion, chopped

1-inch/2.5-cm piece fresh ginger, peeled and finely chopped

1 garlic clove, finely chopped

1 orange bell pepper, seeded and chopped

1 red bell pepper, seeded and chopped

1 tbsp pepper

1 small bunch of fresh chives, snipped

handful of fresh cilantro, chopped

1. Mix the curry paste and soy sauce together in a small bowl and spread over the pork tenderloin. Cover and let marinate in the refrigerator for 1 hour.

2. Meanwhile, preheat the oven to 400°F/200°C. Roast the pork in the preheated oven for 20–25 minutes, or until cooked through. Remove from the oven, then cover with foil and let rest for 15 minutes.

3. Meanwhile, cook the noodles according to the package directions, then drain, rinse under cold running water, and set aside.

4. Heat a wok over medium–high heat, then add the oil. Add the onion, ginger, and garlic and stir-fry for 1–2 minutes. Add the bell peppers and pepper and stir-fry for 2–3 minutes, until tender. Stir in the chives and most of the cilantro.

5. Add the drained noodles to the bell pepper mixture and toss together, until well mixed. Divide among two serving dishes. Slice the pork and arrange it on top of the noodles. Scatter with the remaining cilantro and serve immediately.

Ground Pork Kebabs with Sweet Chili Dipping Sauce

SERVES 4

1 large onion, chopped

2 garlic cloves, crushed

1 lb/450 g ground pork

1 tsp salt

2 tbsp sweet chili dipping sauce, plus extra to serve

handful of fresh cilantro, chopped, plus extra sprigs to garnish (optional)

1 egg

egg-fried rice, to serve

1. Put all the ingredients except the rice in a food processor and process to a thick paste.

2. Divide the pork mixture into eight portions. Using damp hands, squeeze one portion evenly around a flat metal skewer to make eight kebabs. Cover and chill in the refrigerator for at least 1 hour.

3. Heat a ridged grill pan over medium–high heat or preheat a broiler to medium–high. Cook the kebabs, turning occasionally, for 5–6 minutes, or until browned all over and cooked through. Serve immediately on a bed of egg-fried rice with sweet chili dipping sauce and, if desired, garnished with sprigs of fresh cilantro.

Green Lamb Stir-Fry with Noodles and Peanuts

SERVES 4

1 lb/450 g boneless lamb

2 tbsp soy sauce

2 tsp cornstarch

pinch of salt

scant 1 cup chicken stock

1 tbsp Thai fish sauce

3½ oz/100 g Chinese garlic chives or green stalks from 2 bunches scallions

4½ oz/125 g dried egg noodles

3 tbsp peanut oil

¾-inch/2-cm piece galangal or fresh ginger, finely chopped

5 tbsp Green Curry Paste (see page 11)

scant ½ cup dry-roasted peanuts, coarsely chopped

juice of ½ lime

lime slices, to garnish

1. Slice the lamb into 1½ x ½-inch/4 x 1-cm strips and put in a shallow dish. Sprinkle with the soy sauce, cornstarch, and a pinch of salt, tossing well to coat. Cover and let marinate in the refrigerator for 1–24 hours.

2. Combine the stock, fish sauce, and ½ teaspoon of salt. Trim the chives and slice into ¾-inch/2-cm lengths.

3. Cook the noodles according to the package directions. Drain, return to the pan, and toss with 1 tablespoon of the oil.

4. Heat a wok over high heat, then add the remaining oil. Add the lamb and stir-fry for 3 minutes, or until no longer pink. Add the galangal and curry paste and stir for an additional minute. Pour in the stock mixture and stir, until boiling. Add the noodles, tossing to coat with the sauce. Add the chives and stir-fry for a few seconds, until wilted. Sprinkle with the peanuts and lime juice, garnish with slices of lime, and serve immediately.

Red Lamb Curry

SERVES 4

2 tbsp vegetable oil

1 large onion, sliced

2 garlic cloves, crushed

1 lb 2 oz/500 g lean boneless
leg of lamb

2 tbsp Red Curry Paste
(see page 11)

⅔ cup coconut milk

1 tbsp light brown sugar

1 large red bell pepper, seeded and
thickly sliced

½ cup lamb stock or beef stock

1 tbsp Thai fish sauce

2 tbsp lime juice

8 oz/225 g canned water chestnuts,
drained

2 tbsp chopped fresh cilantro

2 tbsp chopped fresh basil,
plus extra leaves to garnish

salt and pepper

cooked jasmine rice, to serve (optional)

1. Heat a wok over high heat, then add the oil. Add the onion and garlic and stir-fry for 2–3 minutes, until softened. Add the lamb and stir-fry the mixture quickly, until lightly browned.

2. Stir in the curry paste and cook for a few seconds, then add the coconut milk and sugar and bring to a boil. Reduce the heat and simmer for 15 minutes, stirring occasionally.

3. Stir in the bell pepper, stock, fish sauce, and lime juice, then cover and simmer for an additional 15 minutes, or until the lamb is tender.

4. Add the water chestnuts, cilantro, and chopped basil and season with salt and pepper to taste. Transfer to serving dishes, then garnish with basil leaves and serve immediately with jasmine rice, if using.

Lamb with Lime Leaves

SERVES 4

1 lb/450 g lean boneless lamb

2 tbsp peanut oil

2 garlic cloves, crushed

4 shallots, chopped

2 lemongrass stalks, sliced

6 fresh kaffir lime leaves

1 tbsp tamarind paste

2 tbsp light brown sugar

2 fresh red Thai chiles, seeded and finely chopped

2½ cups coconut milk

1 cup halved cherry tomatoes

1 tbsp chopped fresh cilantro

cooked Thai fragrant rice, to serve

1. Using a sharp knife, cut the lamb into thin strips or cubes. Set aside until required.

2. Heat a wok over high heat, then add the oil. Add the garlic, shallots, lemongrass, lime leaves, tamarind paste, sugar, and chiles and stir-fry for 2 minutes.

3. Add the lamb to the wok and stir-fry for 5 minutes, tossing well so that the lamb is evenly coated in the spice mixture.

4. Pour the coconut milk into the wok and bring to a boil. Reduce the heat and let simmer for 20 minutes.

5. Add the cherry tomatoes and chopped cilantro to the wok and simmer for 5 minutes. Transfer to serving dishes and serve immediately with rice.

Stir-Fried Lamb with Mint

SERVES 4

generous ⅓ cup fresh mint leaves

2 tbsp vegetable oil

2 garlic cloves, finely sliced

2 fresh red chiles, seeded and cut into
thin strips

1 onion, thinly sliced

1½ tbsp Madras curry paste

1 lb 2 oz/500 g boneless lamb shoulder,
cut into thin strips

2 cups canned baby corn, drained

4 scallions, finely chopped

1 tbsp Thai fish sauce

cooked rice, to serve

1. Coarsely shred the mint leaves and reserve until required. Heat a wok over medium–high heat, then add half the oil. Add the garlic and chiles and cook, until softened. Remove and reserve. Add the onion and cook for 5 minutes, or until softened, then remove and reserve.

2. Heat a separate wok over medium–high heat, then add the remaining oil. Add the curry paste and cook for 1 minute. Add the lamb, in batches if necessary, and cook for 5–8 minutes, or until cooked through and tender.

3. Return the onion to the wok with the baby corn, scallions, mint, and fish sauce. Cook, until heated through. Sprinkle the garlic and chiles over and serve immediately with rice.

Poultry

A universal favorite and infinitely adaptable, chicken shows up in countless dishes on the Thai menu. It was once native to the Southeast Asian jungle and wild birds still exist. Mildly flavored and juicy, chicken is the perfect meat for a wide range of curries, not only the fiery red, green, and yellow classics, but also the slightly milder Chicken with Vegetables and Cilantro Rice.

There are also any number of duck dishes, many emanating from China, where duck was domesticated many centuries ago. With its satisfyingly rich sweet flavor, duck goes well with salty and sour foods, and also stands up well to the incendiary heat of chiles, as in Duck Jungle Curry. For a special occasion try the mouthwatering Crispy Roast Duck with Pickled Plums.

Turkey sometimes appears on the menu, especially in the central region, but it is generally not popular with home cooks because it is too large to be practical and the flesh can sometimes be dry and dense. However, in the West, turkey is sold in portions and can be used in curries and stir-fries in the same way as chicken. It also makes a good substitute for pork because the flesh has a similar texture.

With the Thai insistence on freshness, poultry is always freshly killed and sold with head and feet intact, or, as an absolute guarantee of freshness, purchased live. It is obviously not practical for Western cooks to keep live fowl, but it is worth buying the best quality you can afford.

Green Chicken Curry

SERVES 4

2 tbsp peanut oil

2 tbsp Green Curry Paste
(see page 11)

4 skinless, boneless chicken breasts, cut
into cubes

2 kaffir lime leaves, coarsely torn

1 lemongrass stalk, finely chopped

1 cup coconut milk

16 baby eggplants, halved

2 tbsp Thai fish sauce

fresh Thai basil sprigs and thinly sliced
kaffir lime leaves, to garnish

1. Heat a wok over high heat, then add the oil. Add the curry paste and stir-fry briefly,
   until all the aromas are released.

2. Add the chicken, lime leaves, and lemongrass and stir-fry for 3–4 minutes, until the
   meat is beginning to color. Add the coconut milk and eggplants and simmer gently
   for 8–10 minutes, or until tender.

3. Stir in the fish sauce and serve immediately, garnished with basil sprigs and sliced
   lime leaves.

Red Chicken Curry

SERVES 2–4

6 garlic cloves, chopped

2 red chiles, chopped

2 tbsp chopped lemongrass

1 tsp finely grated lime rind

1 tbsp chopped lime leaves

1 tbsp Red Curry Paste
(see page 11)

1 tbsp coriander seeds

1 tbsp chili oil

4 skinless, boneless chicken breasts,
sliced

1¼ cups coconut milk

1¼ cups chicken stock

1 tbsp soy sauce

⅓ cup ground peanuts

3 scallions, diagonally sliced

1 red bell pepper, seeded and sliced

1 large eggplant, sliced

chopped fresh cilantro, to garnish

cooked rice, to serve

1. Place the garlic, chiles, lemongrass, lime rind, lime leaves, curry paste, and coriander seeds in a food processor and process until the mixture is smooth.

2. Heat a wok over high heat, then add the oil. Add the chicken and garlic mixture and stir-fry for 5 minutes. Add the coconut milk, stock, and soy sauce and bring to a boil. Reduce the heat and cook, stirring, for an additional 3 minutes. Stir in the ground peanuts and simmer for 20 minutes.

3. Add the scallions, bell pepper, and eggplant and simmer, stirring occasionally, for an additional 10 minutes. Garnish with cilantro and serve immediately with rice.

Yellow Chicken Curry

SERVES 4

2 tbsp vegetable oil or peanut oil

2 onions, cut into thin wedges

2 garlic cloves, finely chopped

2 skinless, boneless chicken breasts,
cut into strips

1½ cups baby corn, halved lengthwise

SPICE PASTE

6 tbsp Thai yellow curry paste

⅔ cup plain yogurt

1¾ cups water

handful of fresh cilantro, chopped

handful of fresh Thai basil leaves,
shredded, plus a few whole leaves to
garnish (optional)

1. To make the spice paste, stir-fry the curry paste in a wok for 2–3 minutes, then stir
   in the yogurt, water, and herbs. Bring to a boil, then let simmer for 2–3 minutes.

2. Meanwhile, heat a wok over high heat, then add the oil. Add the onions and
   garlic and stir-fry for 2–3 minutes. Add the chicken and baby corn and stir-fry for
   3–4 minutes, until the meat and corn are tender.

3. Stir in the spice paste and bring to a boil. Let simmer for 2–3 minutes, until heated
   through. Serve immediately, garnished with basil leaves, if using.

Thai Chicken

SERVES 4

6 garlic cloves, coarsely chopped

1 tsp pepper

8 chicken legs

1 tbsp Thai fish sauce

4 tbsp dark soy sauce

fresh ginger, cut into matchsticks,
   to garnish

1. Put the garlic in a mortar, add the pepper and pound to a paste with a pestle. Using a sharp knife, make 3–4 diagonal slashes on both sides of the chicken legs. Spread the garlic paste over the chicken legs and place them in a dish. Add the fish sauce and soy sauce and turn the legs to coat well. Cover with plastic wrap and let marinate in the refrigerator for 2 hours.

2. Preheat the broiler to medium–high. Drain the chicken legs, setting aside the marinade. Put the legs on a broiler rack and cook under the broiler, turning and basting frequently with the reserved marinade, for 20–25 minutes, or until cooked through and tender. The juices should run clear when a skewer is inserted into the thickest part of the meat. Serve immediately, garnished with the ginger.

Chicken with Vegetables and Cilantro Rice

SERVES 4

2 tbsp vegetable oil or peanut oil

1 red onion, chopped

2 garlic cloves, chopped

1-inch/2.5-cm piece fresh ginger, peeled and chopped

2 skinless, boneless chicken breasts, cut into strips

1⅔ cups halved button mushrooms

1¾ cups coconut milk

¾ cup sugar snap peas

1 tbsp Thai fish sauce

2 tbsp soy sauce, plus extra to serve

3 cups rice, cooked and cooled

8 oz/250 g bok choy, torn into large pieces

handful of fresh cilantro, chopped

1. Heat a wok over high heat, then add 1 tablespoon of the oil. Add the onion, garlic, and ginger and sauté for 1–2 minutes.

2. Add the chicken and mushrooms and cook over high heat, until browned. Add the coconut milk, sugar snap peas, fish sauce, and soy sauce and bring to a boil. Let simmer gently for 4–5 minutes, until tender.

3. Heat a separate wok over medium–high heat, then add the remaining oil. Add the onion and cook, until softened but not browned.

4. Add the rice, bok choy, and cilantro, and heat through gently, until the leaves have wilted and the rice is hot. Sprinkle over the soy sauce and serve immediately with the chicken.

Ginger Chicken with Noodles

SERVES 4

2 tbsp vegetable oil or peanut oil

1 onion, sliced

2 garlic cloves, finely chopped

2-inch/5-cm piece fresh ginger, thinly sliced

2 carrots, thinly sliced

4 skinless, boneless chicken breasts, cut into cubes

1¼ cups chicken stock

4 tbsp Thai soy sauce

8 oz/225 g canned bamboo shoots, drained and rinsed

2¾ oz/75 g flat rice noodles

4 scallions, chopped, and 4 tbsp chopped fresh cilantro, to garnish

1. Heat a wok over high heat, then add the oil. Add the onion, garlic, ginger, and carrots and stir-fry for 1–2 minutes, until softened. Add the chicken and stir-fry for 3–4 minutes, until the chicken is cooked through and lightly browned.

2. Add the stock, soy sauce, and bamboo shoots and gradually bring to a boil. Let simmer for 2–3 minutes. Meanwhile, bring a pan of water to a boil, add the noodles, and soak for 6–8 minutes. Drain well. Garnish the noodles with the scallions and cilantro and serve immediately with the chicken stir-fry.

Chicken Curry with Fried Noodles

SERVES 4

2 tbsp peanut oil or vegetable oil,
  plus extra for deep-frying

4 skinless, boneless chicken breasts,
  about 4 oz/115 g each, cut into
  1-inch/2.5-cm cubes

2 red onions, coarsely chopped

5 scallions, coarsely chopped

2 garlic cloves, finely chopped

1 fresh green chile, seeded and
  finely chopped

6 oz/175 g shiitake mushrooms,
  thickly sliced

2 tbsp Green Curry Paste
  (see page 11)

1¾ cups coconut milk

1¼ cups chicken stock

2 fresh kaffir lime leaves

handful of fresh cilantro, chopped

handful of fresh chives, snipped

1 oz/25 g stir-fry rice noodles

cooked rice, to serve (optional)

1. Heat a wok over medium–high heat, then add the oil. Add the chicken cubes, in batches, and stir-fry for 3–4 minutes, or until lightly browned all over. Remove with a slotted spoon, then transfer to a plate and set aside.

2. Add the onions, scallions, garlic, and chile to the wok and stir-fry over medium heat, adding a little more oil if necessary, for 2–3 minutes, or until softened but not browned. Add the mushrooms and stir-fry over high heat for 30 seconds. Return the chicken to the wok.

3. Add the curry paste, coconut milk, stock, and lime leaves and bring gently to a boil, stirring occasionally. Reduce the heat and simmer gently for 4–5 minutes, or until the chicken is tender and cooked through. Stir in the cilantro and chives.

4. Meanwhile, heat a separate wok over high heat, then add the oil for deep-frying and heat to 350–375°F/180–190°C, or until a cube of bread browns in 30 seconds. Divide the noodles into four portions and cook, one portion at a time, for about 2 seconds, until puffed up and crispy. Remove with a slotted spoon and drain on paper towels.

5. Serve the curry with rice, if using, topped with the crispy noodles.

Seven-Spice Chicken with Zucchini

SERVES 4

1 tbsp peanut oil

1 garlic clove, finely chopped

1-inch/2.5-cm piece fresh ginger, finely chopped

1 small fresh red chile, seeded and finely chopped

4 skinless, boneless chicken breasts, cut into thin strips

1 tbsp Thai seven-spice seasoning

1 red bell pepper, seeded and sliced

1 yellow bell pepper, seeded and sliced

2 zucchini, thinly sliced

8 oz/225 g canned bamboo shoots, drained

2 tbsp dry sherry or apple juice

1 tbsp light soy sauce

2 tbsp chopped fresh cilantro, plus extra sprigs to garnish

salt and pepper

cooked rice or egg noodles, to serve

1. Heat a wok over medium–high heat, then add the oil. Add the garlic, ginger, and chile and stir-fry for 30 seconds to release the flavors. Add the chicken and Thai seasoning and stir-fry for 4 minutes, until the chicken has colored all over.

2. Add the bell peppers and zucchini and stir-fry for 1–2 minutes, until slightly softened. Stir in the bamboo shoots and stir-fry for an additional 2–3 minutes, until the chicken is cooked through and tender.

3. Add the sherry, soy sauce, and salt and pepper to taste, and sizzle for 1–2 minutes. Stir in the chopped cilantro, garnish with the cilantro sprigs, and serve immediately with rice.

Chicken and Peanut Curry

SERVES 4

1 tbsp vegetable oil or peanut oil

2 red onions, sliced

2 tbsp Penang curry paste

1¾ cups coconut milk

⅔ cup chicken stock

4 kaffir lime leaves, coarsely torn

1 lemongrass stalk, finely chopped

6 skinless, boneless chicken thighs, chopped

1 tbsp Thai fish sauce

2 tbsp Thai soy sauce

1 tsp light brown sugar

½ cup chopped, unsalted roasted peanuts, plus extra to serve

1 cup coarsely chopped fresh pineapple

6-inch/15-cm piece cucumber, peeled, seeded, and thickly sliced, plus extra to serve

1. Heat a wok over medium–high heat, then add the oil. Add the onions and stir-fry for 1 minute. Add the curry paste and stir-fry for 1–2 minutes.

2. Pour in the coconut milk and stock. Add the lime leaves and lemongrass and let simmer for 1 minute. Add the chicken and gradually bring to a boil. Let simmer for 8–10 minutes, until the chicken is tender.

3. Stir in the fish sauce, soy sauce, and sugar and let simmer for 1–2 minutes. Stir in the peanuts, pineapple, and cucumber and cook for 30 seconds. Serve immediately with peanuts and cucumber.

Shredded Chicken and Mixed Mushrooms

SERVES 4

2 tbsp vegetable oil or peanut oil

2 skinless, boneless chicken breasts

1 red onion, sliced

2 garlic cloves, finely chopped

1-inch/2.5-cm piece fresh ginger, grated

1 cup baby button mushrooms

1 cup halved shiitake mushrooms

1 cup cremini mushrooms, sliced

2–3 tbsp Green Curry Paste
   (see page 11)

2 tbsp Thai soy sauce

4 tbsp chopped fresh parsley

cooked noodles or rice, to serve

1. Heat a wok over medium–high heat, then add the oil. Add the chicken and cook on all sides, until lightly browned and cooked through. Remove with a slotted spoon, shred into even-size pieces, and set aside.

2. Pour off any excess oil, then add the onion, garlic, and ginger and stir-fry for 1–2 minutes, until softened. Add the mushrooms and stir-fry for 2–3 minutes, until they start to brown.

3. Add the curry paste, soy sauce, and shredded chicken to the wok and stir-fry for 1–2 minutes. Stir in the parsley and serve immediately with noodles.

Crispy-Fried Spicy Turkey

SERVES 3–4

1 lb/450 g turkey steaks
2 tbsp Thai fish sauce
2 tbsp light soy sauce
peanut oil, for frying
⅓ cup peanuts, coarsely chopped
4 tbsp chopped Thai basil
lime wedges, to garnish
cooked noodles, to serve

SPICE PASTE
2 tsp coriander seeds
1 tsp cumin seeds
2 tsp white peppercorns
seeds from 3 green cardamom pods
1 tsp sugar
1–2 fresh red chiles, seeded and finely
   chopped
2 garlic cloves, finely chopped

1. To make the spice paste, dry-fry the coriander seeds over medium–high heat, shaking the pan frequently, for 2 minutes, until starting to pop. Remove from the pan, then add the cumin seeds and dry-fry for 30 seconds, until fragrant, being careful not to let them burn. Grind the seeds to a paste with the remaining ingredients, using a mortar and pestle.

2. Pound the turkey steaks with a meat mallet, until they are ¼ inch/5 mm thick. Slice across the grain into ¼ x 1½-inch/5-mm x 4-cm strips and put into a shallow bowl. Rub the spice paste into the meat. Add the fish sauce and soy sauce, tossing to coat. Let marinate at room temperature for 20 minutes.

3. Heat a large wok over high heat, then add enough oil to come to a depth of 1 inch/2.5 cm. Add the turkey and any spice paste from the bowl. Fry for 4 minutes, turning with tongs, until beginning to color. Add the peanuts and fry for an additional minute, or until the turkey is crispy and golden at the edges.

4. Remove with a slotted spoon and drain on paper towels. Turn into a warmed serving dish and sprinkle with the basil. Garnish with lime wedges and serve immediately with noodles.

Duck Jungle Curry

SERVES 4

2 tbsp peanut oil

6 tbsp Green Curry Paste (see page 11)

1 tbsp finely chopped galangal or
fresh ginger

4 tbsp finely chopped shallots

2 tbsp Thai fish sauce

2¼ cups chicken stock

12 oz/350 g boneless, skinless duck
meat, thinly sliced into small strips

4 baby eggplants, quartered

2 small yellow zucchini, thickly sliced
diagonally

8 oz/225 g canned sliced bamboo
shoots, drained and rinsed

juice of 1 lime

handful of Thai basil leaves

cooked rice, to serve

1. Heat a wok over medium–high heat, then add the oil. Add the curry paste,
   galangal, and shallots and stir-fry for 1 minute, until fragrant. Add the fish sauce
   and stock and bring to a boil.

2. Add the duck, eggplants, and zucchini and simmer for about 3 minutes, until the
   vegetables have softened slightly. Add the remaining ingredients and simmer for a
   few more minutes, until the duck is tender.

3. Serve immediately in individual bowls, with rice on the side.

Duck With Chili Jam and Deep-Fried Shallots

SERVES 2–4

2 Barbary duck breasts, weighing about 1 lb 2 oz/500g in total

2 tbsp light soy sauce

3 tbsp Thai fish sauce

2 tsp peanut oil

3 garlic cloves, very finely chopped

¾-inch/2-cm piece galangal or fresh ginger, very finely chopped

½–1 small fresh red chile, seeded and thinly sliced

3 tbsp chili jam

pepper

6 tbsp chopped cilantro, to garnish

cooked rice, to serve

DEEP-FRIED SHALLOTS

peanut oil, for deep-frying

4½ oz/125 g shallots, thinly sliced lengthwise

1. Slice the duck breasts crosswise into thin strips. Put into a shallow bowl in a single layer. Sprinkle with the soy sauce and 2 tablespoons of the fish sauce. Toss to coat, then cover and let marinate in the refrigerator for 2–24 hours, turning once.

2. To make the deep-fried shallots, heat a large wok over high heat, then add enough oil to come to a depth of 1 inch/2.5 cm. Add the shallots and fry for 8–10 minutes, turning with tongs, until golden. Be careful not to let them burn. Remove with tongs and drain on a tray covered with paper towels. The shallots will become crispy as they cool. Pour off the oil and wipe out the wok.

3. Heat the clean wok over high heat, then add the oil. Add the duck and marinade, garlic, galangal, and chile and stir-fry for 3 minutes.

4. Reduce the heat to medium–high and stir in the chili jam, the remaining fish sauce, and the deep-fried shallots. Season with pepper. Stir-fry for 2 minutes, moistening with a little water if necessary, until the sauce is well amalgamated. Sprinkle with the cilantro and serve immediately with rice.

Stir-Fry with Duck and Peas

SERVES 4

1 lb/450 g skinless, boneless duck breasts

3 tbsp peanut oil

6 large scallions, white and green parts separated, diagonally sliced into ¾-inch/2-cm pieces

1 tsp finely chopped fresh ginger

4¾ cups snow peas, sliced in half diagonally

1⅓ cups shelled peas

3 tbsp whole, unpeeled almonds, halved lengthwise

½ cup fresh bean sprouts

cooked noodles, to serve

MARINADE

1 tbsp light brown sugar

3 tbsp lukewarm water

1–2 fresh red chiles, seeded and finely chopped

1 tbsp soy sauce

1 tsp Thai fish sauce

3 tbsp lime juice

1. Combine the marinade ingredients in a bowl, stirring to dissolve the sugar. Slice the duck into bite-size pieces and add to the marinade. Marinate at room temperature for 30 minutes, or overnight in the refrigerator.

2. Heat a wok over high heat, then add the oil. Add the white parts of the scallions and the ginger and stir-fry for a few seconds. Add the duck and marinade and stir-fry for about 5 minutes. When the liquid has reduced slightly, add both types of peas and stir-fry for another 2–3 minutes.

3. Add the almonds, bean sprouts, and green parts of the scallions and stir-fry for a few seconds to heat through. Serve immediately with noodles.

Duck with Mixed Bell Peppers

SERVES 4

1 tbsp vegetable oil or peanut oil

2 duck breasts, skin on

1 onion, sliced

2 garlic cloves, chopped

1 red bell pepper, seeded and chopped

1 green bell pepper, seeded and chopped

1 yellow bell pepper, seeded and chopped

4 tomatoes, peeled, seeded, and chopped

⅔ cup stock

3 tbsp Thai soy sauce

cooked noodles, garnished with chopped scallion, to serve

1. Heat a wok over high heat, then add the oil. Add the duck breasts and cook on one-side, until crispy and brown. Turn and cook, until cooked through. Lift out and keep warm.

2. Pour off any excess fat and stir-fry the onion and garlic for 2–3 minutes, until softened and lightly browned.

3. Add the bell peppers and stir-fry for 2–3 minutes, until tender. Add the tomatoes, stock, and soy sauce and let simmer for 1–2 minutes. Transfer to a serving plate. Slice the duck thickly and arrange on top, spooning any sauce over it. Serve immediately with noodles garnished with chopped scallion.

Crispy Roast Duck and Pickled Plums

SERVES 4

4 boneless duck breasts, about
  6 oz/175 g each

3 scallions, finely chopped

2 garlic cloves, finely chopped

4 tbsp oyster sauce

1 tbsp peanut oil or vegetable oil

cooked noodles, to serve

PICKLED PLUMS

generous ¼ cup superfine sugar

4 tbsp white wine vinegar

1 fresh red chile, seeded and finely
  chopped

½ tsp salt

4 plums, pitted and quartered

1. Use a sharp knife to make diagonal slashes in both directions in the skin of the duck breasts. Mix the scallions, garlic, and oyster sauce together in a small bowl and spread over the duck skin. Cover and let marinate in the refrigerator for 1 hour.

2. Meanwhile, to make the pickled plums, put all the ingredients except the plums in a pan and simmer gently for 10–15 minutes. Add the plums and simmer for an additional 5 minutes, or until just starting to soften. Let cool.

3. Preheat the oven to 400°F/200°C. Heat the oil in a large skillet, then add the duck breasts, skin-side down, and cook for 2–3 minutes, or until browned. Turn over and cook on the other side for 1–2 minutes.

4. Transfer the duck breasts to a roasting pan and roast in the preheated oven for 10–15 minutes, or until just cooked through. Remove from the oven, then cover with foil and let rest for 10 minutes.

5. Serve the duck breasts with the pickled plums and noodles.

Fish and Seafood

With more than 1,500 miles/2,500 km of coastline and extensive inland waterways, Thailand boasts more fish and seafood dishes than any based on meat or poultry. Vast areas of markets are given over to freshwater and sea fish and to every imaginable type of shellfish, from succulent lobsters and crayfish, clams, and scallops, to cockles and mussels, tiny shrimp, and giant freshwater shrimp. Furthermore, almost all Thai dishes are seasoned with Thai fish sauce or shrimp paste, or both.

Flavorsome oily fish, such as mackerel and tuna, are popular, as are dense-fleshed swordfish and barramundi. Their flesh is juicy and firm enough to use for kebabs and curries, while the meaty flavors hold their own with chiles and robust spices.

Deep-fried fish is also popular. Thai cooks do their deep-frying in less oil, at a lower heat, and for longer than we do in the West. The technique produces wonderfully golden, crispy, and almost chewy pieces of fish that are heaven alongside a contrastingly creamy coconut fish curry.

One of the tastiest ways of cooking a whole fish is to wrap it in banana leaves or foil, as in Steamed Sea Bream with Ginger. The fish cooks in its own juices, which are permeated with zesty spices, lime juice, and salty fish sauce.

Freshness is paramount, so fish are kept alive in tanks and pails until purchased, and small shellfish is sold in leakproof plastic bags—no respectable cook would buy anything else.

Green Fish Curry

SERVES 4

2 tbsp vegetable oil

1 garlic clove, chopped

2 tbsp Green Curry Paste
(see page 11)

1 small eggplant, diced

½ cup coconut cream

2 tbsp Thai fish sauce

1 tsp sugar

8 oz/225 g firm white fish, cut into
pieces

½ cup fish stock

2 kaffir lime leaves, finely shredded

about 15 leaves fresh Thai basil

fresh dill sprigs, to garnish

1. Heat a wok over medium heat, then add the oil and heat, until almost smoking.
   Add the garlic and fry, until golden. Add the curry paste and stir-fry for a few
   seconds, then add the eggplant. Stir-fry for about 4–5 minutes, until softened.

2. Add the coconut cream, bring to a boil, and stir, until the cream thickens and
   curdles slightly. Add the fish sauce and sugar to the wok and stir well.

3. Add the fish pieces and stock. Simmer for 3–4 minutes, stirring occasionally,
   until the fish is just tender. Add the lime leaves and basil, then cook for an
   additional 1 minute. Transfer to a large, warmed serving dish, garnish with a few
   sprigs of fresh dill, and serve immediately.

Fish Curry with Rice Noodles

SERVES 4

2 tbsp vegetable oil or peanut oil

1 large onion, chopped

2 garlic cloves, chopped

1 cup button mushrooms

8 oz/225 g monkfish, cut into
   1-inch/2.5-cm cubes

8 oz/225 g salmon fillets, cut into
   1-inch/2.5-cm cubes

8 oz/225 g cod, cut into
   1-inch/2.5-cm cubes

2 tbsp Red Curry Paste
   (see page 11)

1¾ cups coconut milk

handful of fresh cilantro, chopped,
   plus extra to garnish

1 tsp light brown sugar

1 tsp Thai fish sauce

4 oz/115 g rice noodles

3 scallions, chopped

½ cup bean sprouts

a few fresh Thai basil leaves,
   plus extra to garnish

1. Heat a wok over medium–high heat, then add the oil. Add the onion, garlic, and mushrooms and gently sauté, until softened but not browned.

2. Add the fish, curry paste, and coconut milk and bring gently to a boil. Let simmer for 2–3 minutes before adding the cilantro, sugar, and fish sauce. Keep warm.

3. Meanwhile, soak the noodles for 3–4 minutes, until tender, and drain well through a metal colander. Put the colander and noodles over a pan of simmering water. Add the scallions, bean sprouts, and basil and steam on top of the noodles for 1–2 minutes, or until just wilted.

4. Pile the noodles into warmed serving dishes and top with the fish curry. Sprinkle the remaining cilantro and the basil over the top and serve immediately.

Mixed Fish and Coconut Curry

SERVES 4

2 tbsp peanut oil or vegetable oil

6 scallions, cut into 1-inch/2.5-cm lengths

1 large carrot, peeled and cut into thin sticks

½ cup trimmed and sliced green beans

2 tbsp Red Curry Paste (see page 11)

3 cups coconut milk

8 oz/225 g skinned whitefish fillet, such as cod or coley, cut into 1-inch/2.5-cm cubes

8 oz/225 g squid, cleaned and cut into thick rings

8 oz/225 g large shrimp, peeled and deveined

⅓ cup fresh bean sprouts

4 oz/115 g dried rice noodles, cooked according to the package directions and drained

handful of fresh cilantro, chopped

handful of fresh Thai basil leaves, to garnish

1. Heat a wok over medium–high heat, then add the oil. Add the scallions, carrot, and green beans and stir-fry for 2–3 minutes, or until starting to soften.

2. Stir in the curry paste, then add the coconut milk. Bring gently to a boil, stirring occasionally, then reduce the heat and simmer for 2–3 minutes. Add all the seafood and bean sprouts and simmer for 2–3 minutes, or until just cooked through and the shrimp have turned pink.

3. Stir in the cooked noodles and cilantro and cook for 1 minute. Serve immediately, sprinkled with the basil.

Monkfish Kebabs with Red Bell Peppers and Shrimp

SERVES 4

2 red bell peppers, seeded and cut lengthwise into 6 wedges

12 oz/350 g monkfish tail

juice of ½ lime

1 tsp Red Curry Paste (see page 11)

handful of fresh cilantro, chopped, plus a few sprigs to garnish

8 oz/225 g jumbo shrimp, in their shells

cooked rice and stir-fried vegetables (optional), to serve

1. Soak 12 bamboo skewers in cold water for at least 30 minutes. Meanwhile, preheat the broiler to high. Arrange the bell pepper wedges, skin-side up, on a baking sheet and cook under the preheated broiler for 5–8 minutes, or until the skin is blackened. Let cool, then peel off the skin. Cut the flesh into 1-inch/2.5-cm squares.

2. Peel the gray membrane off the monkfish and discard. Cut down either side of the central bone to make two long pieces of fish. Cut into 1-inch/2.5-cm cubes.

3. Mix the lime juice, curry paste, and cilantro together in a large bowl. Add the fish cubes and toss to coat in the mixture. Thread the bell pepper wedges, fish, and shrimp alternately onto the bamboo skewers. Cover and let marinate in the refrigerator for 30 minutes.

4. Heat a ridged grill pan over medium–high heat. Cook the kebabs, turning occasionally, for 4–5 minutes, or until browned all over and cooked through. Garnish with cilantro sprigs and serve immediately on a bed of rice with stir-fried vegetables, if using.

Swordfish Kebabs

SERVES 4

1 lb 9 oz/700 g swordfish steaks,
   cut into bite-size chunks

2 red bell peppers, seeded and cut into
   bite-size squares

1 red onion, cut into bite-size chunks

2 limes

2 garlic cloves, finely chopped

2 tsp chopped fresh ginger

2 fresh red chiles, seeded and finely
   chopped

1 tsp dried lemongrass

2 tbsp sesame oil

handful of fresh cilantro leaves,
   chopped

lime wedges, to serve

1. Put the swordfish, bell peppers, and onion in a nonmetallic dish. Finely grate the rind (without pith) from one of the limes and add to the dish, then squeeze the juice from both limes and add to the dish along with all the remaining ingredients. Stir well, then cover and let marinate in a cool place for 30 minutes–1 hour.

2. Preheat the broiler to high. Thread the swordfish, bell peppers, and onion alternately onto four metal or presoaked wooden skewers. Cook the kebabs under the preheated broiler for 8 minutes, turning halfway through and spooning over any remaining marinade as you do so. Serve immediately with lime wedges.

Steamed Sea Bream with Ginger

SERVES 2

2 sea bream, each weighing about
  14 oz/400 g, cleaned and scaled,
  heads removed

juice of 1 lime

1 tbsp Thai fish sauce

4 scallions, green parts included,
  shredded

2 tbsp peanut oil, plus extra for
  brushing

1¼-inch/3-cm piece fresh ginger, sliced
  into very thin sticks

SPICE PASTE

1 tsp coriander seeds

½ tsp cumin seeds

1 tsp white peppercorns

¼ tsp salt

½-inch/1-cm piece fresh ginger,
  very finely chopped

TO GARNISH

small sprigs of cilantro

1 fresh red chile, seeded and thinly
  sliced

lime wedges

1. Using a sharp knife, make 2 diagonal slashes on each side of the fish. Put in a dish in a single layer. Sprinkle with the lime juice and fish sauce, rubbing the mixture over the skin and into the slashes. Let marinate for 15 minutes.

2. To make the spice paste, dry-fry the coriander seeds over medium–high heat, shaking the pan frequently, for 2 minutes. Remove and reserve, add the cumin seeds to the pan, and dry-fry for 30 seconds, or until fragrant. Combine with the remaining ingredients and grind to a paste using a mortar and pestle. Push the mixture into the slashes of the fish and rub the rest over the skin.

3. Brush two large pieces of thick foil with oil. Place a fish on each piece, along with any spice paste and liquid left in the dish. Sprinkle with the shredded scallion. Make a loose parcel, sealing the edges well. Let stand for 15 minutes. Preheat the oven to 475°F/240°C and put a baking sheet in the oven to heat. Place the fish parcels on the preheated sheet and bake for 10 minutes, then turn and bake for an additional 5 minutes.

4. Meanwhile, heat the oil in a small skillet over medium–high heat. Add the ginger and cook for 1½ –2 minutes, until golden, then drain on crumpled paper towels. Transfer the fish parcels to serving plates. Open the foil, sprinkle the fish with the ginger, garnish with the cilantro, chile, and lime wedges, and serve immediately.

Spiced Tuna in Sweet-and-Sour Sauce

SERVES 4

4 fresh tuna steaks, about
    1 lb 2 oz/500 g in total

¼ tsp pepper

2 tbsp peanut oil

1 onion, diced

1 small red bell pepper, seeded and cut
    into short thin sticks

1 garlic clove, crushed

½ cucumber, seeded and cut into short
    thin sticks

2 pineapple slices, diced

1 tsp finely chopped fresh ginger

1 tbsp brown sugar

1 tbsp cornstarch

1½ tbsp lime juice

1 tbsp Thai fish sauce

1 cup fish stock

lime slices and cucumber ribbons,
    to garnish

1. Sprinkle the tuna steaks with pepper on both sides. Heat a ridged grill pan and
    brush with a little of the oil. Arrange the tuna steaks in the skillet and cook for
    8 minutes, turning once.

2. Meanwhile, heat a wok over medium heat, then add the remaining oil. Add the
    onion, bell pepper, and garlic and cook gently for 3–4 minutes to soften.

3. Remove the wok from the heat and stir in the cucumber, pineapple, ginger, and
    sugar. Blend the cornstarch with the lime juice and fish sauce, then stir into the
    stock and add to the vegetable mixture. Stir over medium heat, until boiling, then
    cook for 1–2 minutes, or until thickened and clear.

4. Spoon the sauce over the tuna and serve immediately, garnished with slices of lime
    and cucumber ribbons.

Spicy Seafood Stew

SERVES 4

7 oz/200 g squid, cleaned and tentacles
  discarded

1 lb 2 oz/500 g firm whitefish fillet,
  preferably monkfish or halibut

1 tbsp corn oil

4 shallots, finely chopped

2 garlic cloves, finely chopped

2 tbsp Green Curry Paste
  (see page 11)

2 small lemongrass stems,
  finely chopped

1 tsp shrimp paste

generous 2 cups coconut milk

7 oz/200 g jumbo shrimp,
  peeled and deveined

12 clams in shells, cleaned

8 fresh basil leaves, finely shredded,
  plus a few whole leaves, to garnish

cooked rice, to serve

1. Using a sharp knife, cut the squid body cavities into thick rings and the whitefish into bite-size chunks.

2. Heat a large wok over medium–high heat, then add the oil. Add the shallots, garlic, and curry paste and stir-fry for 1–2 minutes. Add the lemongrass and shrimp paste, then stir in the coconut milk and bring to a boil.

3. Reduce the heat, until the liquid is simmering gently, then add the squid, whitefish, and shrimp to the wok and simmer for 2 minutes.

4. Add the clams and simmer for an additional 1 minute, or until the clams have opened. Discard any clams that remain closed.

5. Sprinkle the shredded basil leaves over the stew. Transfer to serving plates, then garnish with whole basil leaves and serve immediately with rice.

Marinated Fried Scallops

SERVES 4

16 large shucked scallops with corals
1 tbsp peanut oil
1 tbsp toasted sesame oil
squeeze of lime juice

TO GARNISH
1 tbsp chopped fresh cilantro
1 tbsp chopped fresh mint
lime wedges

MARINADE
juice of 1 lime
1 fresh red chile, seeded and
    thinly sliced
2 tsp light soy sauce
2 tsp Thai fish sauce
1 tsp sugar
¼ tsp pepper

1. Put the scallops in a shallow dish. Combine the marinade ingredients and pour over the scallops, tossing to coat. Cover and let marinate in the refrigerator for 30 minutes–2 hours.

2. Heat a wok over high heat, then add the peanut oil and sesame oil. Add the scallops and stir-fry with any juices from the marinade for 4–5 minutes, until cooked through. Sprinkle with a squeeze of lime juice. Turn into a warmed serving dish along with any cooking juices, then garnish with the cilantro, mint, and lime wedges and serve immediately.

Shrimp with Coconut Rice

SERVES 4

1 cup dried Chinese mushrooms

1 tbsp vegetable oil or peanut oil

6 scallions, chopped

scant ½ cup dry unsweetened coconut

1 fresh green chile, seeded and chopped

generous 1 cup jasmine rice

⅔ cup fish stock

1¾ cups coconut milk

12 oz/350 g cooked, peeled shrimp, thawed if frozen

6 sprigs fresh basil

1. Place the mushrooms in a small bowl, cover with hot water, and set aside to soak for 30 minutes. Drain, then cut off and discard the stalks and slice the caps.

2. Heat a wok over medium–high heat, then add the oil. Add the scallions, coconut, and chile and stir-fry for 2–3 minutes, until lightly browned. Add the mushrooms and stir-fry for 3–4 minutes.

3. Add the rice and stir-fry for 2–3 minutes, then add the stock and bring to a boil. Reduce the heat and add the coconut milk. Let simmer for 10–15 minutes, until the rice is tender. Stir in the shrimp and basil, heat through, and serve immediately.

Shrimp Noodle Bowl

SERVES 4

1 bunch of scallions

2 celery stalks

1 red bell pepper

7 oz/200 g rice vermicelli noodles

2 tbsp peanut oil

½ cup unsalted peanuts

1 fresh Thai chile, sliced

1 lemongrass stalk, crushed

1¾ cups fish stock or chicken stock

scant 1 cup coconut milk

2 tsp Thai fish sauce

12 oz/350 g cooked, peeled jumbo
   shrimp

salt and pepper

3 tbsp chopped fresh cilantro,
   to garnish

1. Trim the scallions and celery and thinly slice diagonally. Seed and thinly slice the bell pepper.

2. Put the noodles into a bowl, cover with boiling water, and let stand for 4 minutes, until tender. Drain.

3. Heat a wok over medium–high heat, then add the oil. Add the peanuts and stir-fry for 1–2 minutes, until golden. Lift out with a slotted spoon. Add the sliced scallions, celery, and bell pepper and stir-fry over high heat for 1–2 minutes. Add the chile, lemongrass, stock, coconut milk, and fish sauce and bring to a boil.

4. Stir in the shrimp, then return to a boil, stirring. Season with salt and pepper to taste, then add the noodles. Serve immediately in warmed bowls, sprinkled with the cilantro.

Egg-Fried Rice with Shrimp and Bell Peppers

SERVES 4

generous 1 cup jasmine rice

1 tbsp peanut oil or vegetable oil

2 scallions, finely chopped

2 eggs, beaten

handful of fresh cilantro, chopped, plus extra sprigs to garnish

SHRIMP AND BELL PEPPERS

4 tbsp peanut oil or vegetable oil

2 fresh red chiles, coarsely chopped

6 scallions, coarsely chopped

12 oz/350 g cooked, peeled shrimp

2 oz/55 g creamed coconut, chopped and dissolved in ⅔ cup boiling water

juice of ½ lemon

6 fresh Thai basil leaves, torn

1 tbsp Thai fish sauce

1 red bell pepper, seeded and cut into strips

1. Cook the rice according to the package directions. Rinse under cold running water, then fluff up with a fork and let cool completely.

2. Heat a wok over medium–high heat, then add the oil. Add the scallions and stir-fry for 30 seconds. Add the rice and stir-fry for 1–2 minutes, or until heated through. Push all the rice to one side of the wok and tilt the pan to let any oil run to the opposite side. While still tilted, add the eggs and cook over medium heat, stirring constantly, for 2–3 minutes, or until set. Return the wok to a level position, then add the cilantro and stir the rice through the cooked eggs. Remove from the heat but keep the rice warm in the wok.

3. For the shrimp and bell peppers, heat a separate wok over medium–high heat, then add most of the oil. Add the chiles and scallions and stir-fry for 1–2 minutes, or until just tender. Add the shrimp, coconut mixture, lemon juice, basil, and fish sauce and bring gently to a boil, stirring occasionally, to ensure that the shrimp are heated through.

4. Heat a small skillet over high heat, then add the remaining oil. Add the bell pepper and stir-fry for 1–2 minutes, or until sizzling and lightly browned. Stir into the chile-shrimp mixture, garnish with cilantro, and serve immediately with the rice.

Chili Shrimp with Garlic Noodles

SERVES 4

7 oz/200 g cooked, peeled, and
   deveined jumbo shrimp

4 tbsp sweet chili dipping sauce

4 tbsp peanut oil or vegetable oil

4 scallions, chopped

2 oz/55 g snow peas, trimmed and
   halved diagonally

1 tbsp Red Curry Paste (see page 11)

1¾ cups canned coconut milk

2 oz/55 g canned, drained bamboo
   shoots

⅓ cup fresh bean sprouts

GARLIC NOODLES

4 oz/115 g dried medium egg noodles

2 garlic cloves, crushed

handful of fresh cilantro, chopped

1. Toss the shrimp with the chili sauce in a bowl. Cover and set aside.

2. Heat a wok over medium–high heat, then add half the oil. Add the scallions and snow peas and stir-fry for 2–3 minutes. Add the curry paste and stir well. Pour in the coconut milk and bring gently to a boil, stirring occasionally. Add the bamboo shoots and bean sprouts and cook, stirring, for 1 minute. Stir in the shrimp and chili sauce, reduce the heat, and simmer for 1–2 minutes, or until just heated through.

3. Meanwhile, for the garlic noodles, cook the noodles according to the package directions. Drain and return to the pan.

4. Heat the remaining oil in a small, nonstick skillet, then add the garlic and stir-fry over high heat for 30 seconds. Add to the drained noodles with half the cilantro and toss together, until well mixed.

5. Transfer the chili shrimp mixture to four warmed serving bowls. Serve immediately, garnished with the remaining cilantro, with the garlic noodles.

Shrimp and Pineapple Curry

SERVES 4

½ fresh pineapple

1¾ cups coconut cream

2 tbsp Red Curry Paste
(see page 11)

2 tbsp Thai fish sauce

2 tsp sugar

12 oz/350 g jumbo shrimp, peeled
and deveined

2 tbsp chopped cilantro

steamed jasmine rice, to serve

1. Peel the pineapple and chop the flesh. Put the coconut cream, pineapple, curry paste, fish sauce, and sugar in a pan and heat, until almost boiling.

2. Add the shrimp and chopped cilantro to the pan and simmer for 3 minutes, or until the shrimp are cooked and have turned a bright pink color.

3. Serve immediately with rice.

Stir-Fried Squid with Hot Black Bean Sauce

SERVES 4

1 lb 10 oz/750 g squid, cleaned and
   tentacles discarded

1 large red bell pepper, seeded

scant 1 cup snow peas

1 head bok choy

1 tbsp peanut oil

1 small fresh red Thai chile, chopped

1 garlic clove, finely chopped

1 tsp grated fresh ginger

2 scallions, chopped

BLACK BEAN SAUCE

3 tbsp black bean sauce

1 tbsp Thai fish sauce

1 tbsp rice wine or dry sherry

1 tbsp dark soy sauce

1 tsp light brown sugar

1 tsp cornstarch

1 tbsp water

1. Cut the squid body cavities into quarters lengthwise. Use the tip of a small, sharp knife to score a diamond pattern into the flesh without cutting all the way through. Pat dry with paper towels.

2. Cut the bell pepper into long, thin slices. Cut the snow peas in half diagonally. Coarsely shred the bok choy.

3. To make the sauce, mix the black bean sauce, fish sauce, rice wine, soy sauce, and sugar together in a bowl. Blend the cornstarch with the water and stir into the other ingredients in the bowl. Reserve the mixture until required.

4. Heat a wok over medium–high heat, then add the oil. Add the chile, garlic, ginger, and scallions and stir-fry for 1 minute. Add the bell pepper slices and stir-fry for 2 minutes.

5. Add the squid and stir-fry over high heat for an additional 1 minute. Stir in the snow peas and bok choy and stir for an additional 1 minute, or until wilted.

6. Stir in the sauce ingredients and cook, stirring continuously, for 2 minutes, or until the sauce thickens and clears. Serve immediately.

Index